D0306621

LOOK OUT FOR THE CHURCH

LOOK OUT FOR THE CHURCH

A Long Range Forecast

by

EDWARD H. PATEY
Dean of Liverpool

LUTTERWORTH PRESS
LONDON

First published 1970

Lutterworth Press,
4 Bouverie Street, London, E.C.4

7188 1371 5

Printed in Great Britain
by Cox & Wyman Ltd.,
London, Reading and Fakenham

CONTENTS

ACKNOWLEDGMENTS

Biblical quotations are from the Jerusalem Bible © 1966 Darton, Longman & Todd Limited and Doubleday & Company Inc. and are used by permission.

Standing in the Rain is quoted by permission of Sydney Carter and Essex Music Limited.

The lines by the Rev. Fred Kaan from *Magnificat Now* are taken from *Pilgrim Praise* and are quoted by permission.

The quotations from *Working with Unattached Youth* are by permission of Routledge and Kegan Paul.

Grateful thanks are also extended to the publishers of the other copyright material quoted in the course of this book.

1

OUTLOOK UNSETTLED

HAD I BEEN ALLOWED to choose in which period of history I would be a minister of the Gospel, I would still choose the present time. If it is a difficult time, it is also one of immense exhilaration and hope. If it is no longer easy to rely on the older policies, there is a thrilling new spirit of exploration to take its place. For I am convinced that we shall emerge from the theological ferment of this age knowing that, far from being dead, the God revealed to us in Jesus Christ is marvellously alive and active in our world. The Christian faith will have more to give to the future of man than it has given to its past. But the vehicle through which that faith must be given to the world, the Christian Church, has a stormy passage ahead. If we can face the long-range weather forecast with confidence, we must also recognize that in the immediate future the outlook is unsettled.

This book is a personal view of the Christian task today. It makes no greater claim than that. It comes out of the experience of a ministry which, in the first half, was mainly concerned with work amongst young people, and which has, latterly, been involved in the life of the two new cathedrals of Coventry and Liverpool. Both growing boys and girls and newly built cathedrals tend to create a dissatisfaction with the past and with the *status quo*. Both compel a forward look. Something of this restlessness with what is, and a hopefulness for what is to be, will be detected in the pages which follow.

Whilst this book was being written, the leaders of the World Church went to Uppsala, and the Anglican bishops went to Lambeth. Neither meeting produced fruits of great significance, but their deliberations are noted from time to time in these pages. More significantly, the Pope issued the Encyclical *Humanae Vitae*, and the Russians invaded Czechoslovakia. Both events created reactions of great importance. The first men walked on the moon, and the Church of England refused to step forward into unity with the Methodists. Everywhere students were in revolt against authorities. And all the time the institutional Church continued to lose ground. Yet the claims of Christ are taken as seriously as ever. Some of the deepest insights of the Bible are being rediscovered with a new clarity in this time of crisis and change.

CRISIS OF AUTHORITY

For those who remain within the fold of the Church, the crisis facing them is increasingly that of loyalty to authority. There have always been radicals and rebels in the Church. Sometimes they have been thrown out and branded as heretics. Sometimes they have fulfilled the more useful function of remaining in the fold and acting as gadflys. But the rank and file have been undisturbed by these deviations. In one way or another, the Church has maintained discipline by an appeal to some overriding authority.

In the Churches of the Reformation this authority has resided in the Bible as the Word of God. If a dogma can be proved from scripture, it is true and must be believed. If it is not found in Scripture, it is not 'necessary to salvation'. The Bible was the divine litmus paper, always to be relied upon to give the acid test. This authority has been dramatically weakened during the past century.

First of all, the palaeontologists began to show that the creation stories of Genesis could not be taken as serious history. Then followed an intensive era of Biblical criticism undertaken primarily by Christians themselves. The authorship of many books, both in the Old Testament and in the New, was thrown in doubt. Historical narratives were shown to be extensively coloured by the subjective views of the writers. The comparative study of religion suggested that some of the Biblical insights were not exclusive to the 'Word of God' but could be paralleled in other traditions. A careful examination of the way in which oral tradition was passed down from one generation to another caused scholars to cast doubt on the historicity of some of the key events in the life of Christ as recorded in the Gospels.

There remains today a wide interest in the Bible. New translations have a ready sale; and there are hundreds of books about the Bible published every year. The cinema, in its despair over diminishing box-office receipts, turns again and again to the Scriptures for scripts which will attract the public. But the authority of the Bible as the ultimate last word has been jeopardized beyond hope of repair by the work of modern scholarship and investigation.

BIBLE SCEPTICS

Nor is this scepticism of Biblical authority confined to scholars. It has invaded the class-room and Sunday school. Researchers, like Dr. Ronald Goldman and Mr. Harold Loukes, have shown that children are ready to accept Scripture as if it were literal history up to the age of 11. Then they suddenly discover that what they are taught in their Bible lesson or in church on Sundays does not harmonize with what they are learning in their other academic disciplines. If they have to decide between the physics master and the religious knowledge teacher, the chances are they will decide to rely on the scientist. Most teenagers in Britain would endorse the sentiments of the cynic in Gershwin's opera:

> It ain't necessarily so.
> It ain't necessarily so.
> De t'ings dat you' li'ble to read in de Bible
> It ain't necessarily so.

This does not mean that Biblical fundamentalism is dead. It fights a vigorous battle against Biblical criticism, aided by all the technology of mass communication and high pressure salesmanship. But the truth is that the day is passing when anybody can expect to get an effective response simply on the basis of treating the Bible as literal truth.

VENTILATION OF IDEAS

It is not only those manifestations of Christianity which see authority focused on the Bible which face a crisis today. Those ecclesiastical bodies which place absolute authority on the dogmas and disciplines of the Church face a similar dilemma. What criticism has done to Biblical authoritarianism, education and public discussion have done to ecclesiastical authoritarianism. The liberalizing policy, initiated by Pope John XXIII and continued under his successor in the debates within the Vatican Council, enabled a public ventilation of ideas which has already made a profound impact within the Roman Catholic Church and beyond. Debates about basic policy and dogmas, which once took place behind closed doors, have now been held with the whole world in the auditorium. The laity, who once were treated by the hierarchy in a 'not in front of the children' fashion, can now join in the discussion, and have been found to have very definite ideas of their own.

The public controversy following the Papal Encyclical, *Humanae Vitae*, showed very clearly that the crisis which Protestants had already faced in relation to Biblical authority had now shifted ground. Rome had become the battle-ground for the old contest of liberalism versus orthodoxy. What had started as a discussion on birth control became a major crisis of authority. And the dilemma in which the bishops found themselves illustrated the nature of the crisis with a startling clarity for all the world to see. They found themselves placed in the awkward predicament of having to maintain loyalty to the authority of the Pope on the one hand, and of not breaking faith as the pastors of their clergy and laity on the other.

But those who belong to other Churches have no reason to feel superior in the face of the Roman Catholics' public debate. In one form or another, the debate continues in every part of Christendom. There can be no future in fundamentalism, whether Biblical or ecclesiastical. This concept of authority belongs to an age that is fast passing away.

We see further instance of this changing attitude towards authority in the diminishing role of the Church in society and in the weakening influences of the clergy throughout the western world. Everyone in Western Europe is familiar with the picture of the old parish church in the centre of the village or small town. Even today the church in some places may give an illusion that it is at the hub of things. Once upon a time it really was the centre, not only for the worship of God on Sundays and Holy Days, but for education, health, welfare, art, drama, music, and all kinds of recreation as well. In Great Britain, this ideal picture (in so far as it ever existed in reality) was shattered by the Industrial Revolution. The growth of heavily populated urban areas soon edged the church out of its position at the centre, even though great reformers like the early Methodists travelled the country indefatigably trying to keep the Gospel alive and relevant to ordinary people in their daily lives.

Yet the Church was able to hold on to much of the initiative in social action right into the nineteenth century. Much of today's social work, both in the statutory and voluntary services, is built on foundations laid by great Christians of the last century, such as William Booth, Dr. Barnardo and Josephine Butler.

This is also true in education. The National Secularist Society may urge the abolition of religious teaching in the

English state school (which might even be a good thing for the Christian cause), but it was the Christian Church which first gave immense thought and care to education long before the State felt that it had any obligation here.

Some of our most famous youth organizations have lately been celebrating jubilees and centenaries. Church-centred bodies such as the Y.M.C.A. and the Boys' Brigade were pioneering leisure-time activities for young people when the rest of the community was content either to exploit the young, or to tolerate them so long as they did not make a nuisance of themselves. Long before the modern conception of the Welfare State was born, the Church distributed relief to the poor and provided accommodation for the elderly and infirm.

In countless ways the clergy and lay officials had contact with the community, meeting people with practical sympathy and understanding of their needs. This practical action commended the Church even to those who could not accept or understand her dogma, and who had no wish to join in her worship. The Church was seen to be a body which cared about people and their needs.

CHANGING ROLE OF THE CHURCH

The situation today is different. More and more things which provided the Church with a meeting-point with the community have been taken over, first by other voluntary bodies and societies, more recently by the State itself. Successive acts of legislation have put education, health, public assistance, and the care of children, the unmarried mother, the young delinquent and the elderly, into the hands of the community as a whole, either through Government departments or through local authorities. It is no longer the minister or vicar who comes to the door to see about the things which most deeply affect the life of the family. It is the child care officer, the probation officer, the psychiatric social worker, the health visitor, the youth officer, the man from the Ministry of Social Security. There have sprung up a whole army of men and women highly trained in the field of social welfare.

So the Church looks more and more as though it is being thrown back, either into purveying a particular commodity called 'religion', or in providing an uplifting social club for the leisure-time of the diminishing number of people who care for that kind of thing.

OUTLOOK UNSETTLED?

Certainly the concept of God is in a precarious state in England today, and there is probably little difference between England and the rest of the Christian West. On the intellectual plane, those who uphold a belief in God are fighting a rear-guard action against an army of new ideas. On the practical level, the idea of God makes less and less difference to the ordinary conditions of men's lives. Even if God is not dead, for all practical purposes He makes so little difference that it does not matter whether He is alive or not.

Yet the future outlook, even if unsettled, is not without hope. For all its ferment, the mid twentieth century may, in the light of history, prove to be one of the great ages of faith. But it will be a faith, not in the old orthodoxies, but in the emergence of a new understanding of the Gospel in the light of our contemporary debate and experience.

We shall emerge from these times with a simpler Gospel. Much dogmatic elaboration, once considered essential but now seen to have been close to superstition and magic, will be discarded. Orthodoxy will not demand that we believe so much as once we did. There are many points upon which we may have to be content to be agnostic. But what we do believe will have a new intensity and relevance. And the person of Jesus Christ, the 'Man for others', will speak to us of God today with a new power and directness.

This is already beginning to be reflected in a worship which is more meaningful and an ethic which is more concerned with real questions. And since the reappraisal of religious truth cuts across all denominational barriers, it makes its own special contribution to Christian unity.

2

OUTLOOK ON THE BIBLE

IT IS THE INSISTENT message of the Bible that man's relationship with his God and his relationship with his brother are inextricably linked.

THE HERE AND NOW

It is because the ordinary Christian congregation has failed to make this simple point clear, that men and women have increasingly turned away from the Church, finding it an irrelevant waste of time. For the tens who are sceptical of Christianity because they cannot accept its intellectual claims, there are hundreds who despair of Christianity because it does not appear to have anything to do with real life. To become a Christian, they believe, is to join a 'holy club' for the propagation of archaic practices and milk-and-water fellowship.

Any attempt to present the Christian Gospel to modern man must begin at the relevant point of need. We must begin with the here and now before we can speak of the eternal dimension. This is why the traditional homiletic method cuts so little ice except with those who are 'sermon-hardened'. Traditionally, we have begun with the Bible text. This has been expounded in terms of its meaning and context. When we have discussed what is meant by 'once upon a time', it is then 'applied' to the modern world situation. But long before the application is reached, the congregation has absented itself in mind, if not in body.

JESUS' EARLY LIFE

It is remarkable how little time in the life of Jesus was taken up with the things which the Evangelists thought it important to record. The main Gospel narratives deal with less than three years in the life of a man who lived until He was past 30. Apart from the birth stories (of doubtful historical value) and the one incident at the age of 12, we know nothing about the childhood and young manhood of Jesus of Nazareth.

The modern biographer would wish to probe as deeply as the evidence allowed into the parentage and early environment of his subject. Relations, teachers, school-mates, and a host of others would be questioned to discover significant influences on the development of the growing boy. Achievement in the class-room, on the sports field, and in the early apprentice days in the workshop, would all be recorded and analysed. And the friendships and interests of young adulthood would all be spelled out to complete the picture.

In the story of Jesus we know about none of these things. The greater part of His human life is shrouded in the mystery of the hidden years. Religious novelists and artists can let their imaginations run riot without fear of con-tradiction. For the Gospels are not biographies in the modern sense. The full record was not their concern.

THE DIVINE PLAN

Yet the fact of the hidden years remains important for our understanding of the Christian revelation, For, if Christians are right in their claim that in some unique way the life of Jesus reflects the nature of God Himself, it cannot be that a single moment in that life is without significance in the divine plan. The significance of these years lies precisely in their hiddenness.

When God wanted to reveal Himself to man, He did so in the life of a Jewish workman, the greater part of whose life is lost in history. For two and a half years He went about teaching and doing good. In this He attracted much public attention. The events in which His early life culminated were destined to turn the whole world upside down. But the notable thing about the 29 years prelude to the public ministry is that they were so ordinary as not to be worth recording. God inaugurates the perfect revelation of Himself to man by an act of such complete identification with the human situation that for a quarter of a century it remained entirely unnoticed.

JESUS' MINISTRY

When we turn to the records of the Ministry of Jesus, we see how essential His long years of hidden apprenticeship were. Pious meditation (not unexpectedly, primarily by the clergy) has concentrated on the idea of Jesus Christ as the great High Priest. This is a profound truth, but it needs to be balanced by the concept of the great High Layman. For the impact that Jesus made in the streets and lanes of Palestine during His two-and-a-half years of active ministry was that He was not the conventional idea of the priest or the professionally religious.

The authority with which He spoke was quite unlike that of the accepted religious teachers of the day. In a society where religious orthodoxy mattered so much, He stood out for His unorthodox approach to many of the most cherished pietisms. His first care was for the ordinary man and woman in need. People flocked to Him because (unlike the priest and levite in the parable) He cared about people and their everyday problems more than He cared about rules and regulations. So He healed the broken in body and the crazed in mind. It was a practical ministry of the everyday. It was the equivalent, in terms of the Palestine of the first century, of the work today of Christian Aid, Oxfam, War on Want, the Samaritans, the Simon Community, and everyone else who believes that dogma and uplift make no sense to people with empty bellies and bruised bodies.

When, in the firm context of this practical down-to-earth ministry, He began to point men and women to their deeper needs, He did so in a language which they could understand. Never was there a less 'churchy' religious teacher. Not only was the world His parish, but the illustrations He used to drive His points home all came out of the experience of every day. His imagery was neither high-faluting nor ecclesiastical. It was the language of 'Coronation Street' and 'The Archers' rather than of Westminster or Geneva. His parables were drawn from the domestic, social, and industrial life of the community in which He lived. People knew that He understood them. 'He could tell what a man had in him' (Jn. 2: 25).

CONCERN FOR HUMANITY

For this reason the first task of the Church is to display a concern for humanity. The Church must learn to share in the ordinariness of the hidden years. It is because Christians so often give the impression that God is only interested in religion, that the Church appears to be increasingly a narrow and specialized community of people whose queer tastes lead them to be interested in things ecclesiastical. All too often the advertised programmes of church activities confirm this impression. The notices in the church porch, the material in the parish magazine, the subjects chosen by speakers to church fellowships or the men's and women's societies, all confirm this image of a church busily involved in contemplating its own navel. Often there seems little evidence that the heart of the good news is that the Word became flesh and dwelt amongst men.

Perhaps the new lease of life evident in the Humanist group in England today is evidence of the inability of the Christian Church to make it clear that because it claims

to love God it also must love people. Of course, there are
old-fashioned fundamentalist Humanists just as there are
old-fashioned fundamentalist Christians. These are the
people who become so imprisoned in their 'positions'
that dogma and principle are more important to them
than men and women. But many Humanists today
meet together, not primarily to uphold their prepared
positions, but because they have a deep concern for the
welfare of their fellow-men. They hate all ethical and social
systems which make it more difficult for people to be
fully human. They are deeply concerned with such
problems as abortion, divorce, race relations, and
education, for precisely the same reasons as Christians
should be (but not always are) concerned with these
things.

When clergy are short of material for their church
magazines, or ministers want to hit the headlines with a
'powerful' sermon, they often choose to fulminate against
the materialism or the worldliness of our times. They
point to the Bingo queues, or the money spent on alcohol
or gambling, and quote that man cannot live by bread
alone. Their diatribes are well-meaning, and contain
some element of truth. Yet we have not learned the most
elementary lesson in evangelism if we fail to convince all
men and women of good will that we go along with them
in their concern for the welfare of people and the betterment of the world.

Christians must begin (as Jesus did in the hidden 29
years) firmly in the world. The first stage of the Christian
ministry must be the meeting of the world's needs; not as
a sprat with which to catch more spiritual mackerel, but
in obedience to the vision of the God who so loved the
world that He sent His Son into it.

The truth is that, far from being too 'worldly', the
Church does not seem to take the world with the same
seriousness as Jesus did. We should begin by outdoing the
Humanists on their own ground: not in a spirit of competi-

tion but because this is the divine starting point. We must show that the Christian is the true Humanist.

Does this mean that the Christian faith today can only be seen as one of a number of systems concerned with human betterment? Do not Christians have some special insight to bring to the panaceas of modern Humanism?

HEART OF THE STORY

The story of Jesus Christ did not finish with the picture of a man going about doing good and healing disease amongst the people. The heart of the story lies not in good works but in the Cross. It is here that the four evangelists focus their main attention. To them this was the whole point of the story. But has the Cross still its ancient power today? Or is this the part of the story we must discard if we are to be up-to-date and meet the needs of the modern world?

To answer these questions we need to see the Bible as a whole. For the Old Testament also has its hidden years. The old controversies about the historicity of the early chapters of Genesis are now long past. The stories of Adam and Eve, Cain and Abel, and the Tower of Babel, cannot be used to prove the origins of human life, or of the ordering of society.

RELATIONSHIPS

Starting with the assertion that God intended the world to be an experiment in right relationships, the Bible begins by exploring how self-seeking has frustrated this purpose. Not only in sex (Adam and Eve), industry (Cain and Abel), and politics (Babel), but in the whole of life men and women need to rediscover the art of living together with God and with one another. Failure to do so is clearly seen to have its roots in selfishness. This is the idolatry which puts self-seeking in the centre of the scene which is God's rightful place. How man can be brought to his senses is the question which the Bible poses and seeks to answer.

Man's relationship with man had failed because of his broken relationship with God. What was needed was a kind of controlled laboratory experiment in the double dimension of relationships between man and his neighbour and man and his God. Abraham and his descendants were called to provide this experiment. The Covenant was the idea in which this was to be worked out. Like all laboratory workers, they were not just experimenting in right relationships on their own behalf. Abraham was told that 'all the tribes of the earth shall bless themselves by you' (Gen. 12: 3). The privilege of being chosen for this experimental job involved far-reaching responsibilities. Like priests, they were only being given special insights in order that they might impart them to others.

In this ancient Covenant concept we already see what the Christian Church was to become. Already the experience of Abraham and Moses raises some uncomfortable questions for the modern Church. We shall return to some of these later, but it might be well to pause at this stage and ask how much the local congregation today considers itself to be a laboratory of relationships.

Is the local church the place where the double dimension of man's relationship with his fellow-men and with his God are worked out in a whole variety of experiments? Or is it seen by most people to be a society (largely pseudo-middle-class) providing religious diversions for those whose spare-time interests are largely ecclesiastical? It is certainly true that the church of the future will have to be less complex both in its dogmatic requirements and in its organization and practice. It is equally certain that this basic Old Testament insight of the church as a laboratory for right relationships will have to be taken with increasing seriousness.

SOCIAL RESPONSIBILITY

The Law Books (such as Numbers and Leviticus) link man's response to God with his social responsibility in the community. They include regulations about public health, sanitation, quarantine, finance, loans, property rights, weights and measures, nature conservancy, and industrial safety regulations. Man's relationship with God brings him face to face with concerns which today would not be considered to be the business of the Church, but of the local authority, the trades unions, the social and health services.

The same truths are reflected in the writings of the prophets, a remarkable body of men, who lived out their lives in the rough and tumble of political, economic, and social concerns. Where they differed from the ordinary run of men was in their ability to read into every head-line situation signs of the mercy and judgment of God.

Amos, for example, is the forerunner of Merfyn Temple fasting in Westminster Abbey as a protest against the luxury of the copes and communion silver in a world where millions starve. He saw as clearly as anyone in the Old Testament that the only right response to a God who cares for His world is for His people to care for that world too.

Many of the prophets, Isaiah, Jeremiah and Ezekiel among them, were engaged in discovering the will of God for a small nation tossed backwards and forwards on the tempestuous sea of Middle East power politics. Their relationship with God inevitably involved them in 'meddling with politics'.

RACE

But it was on the question of race that the Old Testament experiment in right relationships met its biggest and (in the end) insoluble problem. Abraham was called to create a laboratory community. They were to be the chosen people; but they were to be chosen not for their own sakes, but for the sake of all mankind. Yet to give one nation a special sense of responsibility was to run the risk of blinding it to its responsibilities to others. History is full of instances of people whose sense of destiny led them into a blind and selfish imperialism.

The big quest of the Old Testament was for an understanding of the right relationship of this 'holy nation' to the people of other races. A too great preoccupation with the affairs of this world leads to a humanism in which God is a cypher, or totally ignored; too great a concern for the inner life of holiness can lead to introspection and smug self-conceit. This was the Old Testament problem. Anxious to hold tightly on to their privileged position as God's chosen people, the Hebrew leaders were continually warning against the dangers of fraternization with the surrounding peoples. The final collapse (so it seemed) of this privileged people came when the Exile into Babylon brought with it a predictable increase of nationalism at its most uncompromising.

There were voices raised against this policy. A few men saw that the call to be an experiment in relationships would be jeopardized by such narrowness of outlook. True religion is concerned with creating relationships, not with restricting them. One such man was the unknown writer of the book of Ruth, a tract which boldly declared, at a time of extreme jingoism, that the great national hero, King David, actually had foreign blood coursing through his veins. Another was the writer of the Book of Jonah, who presented a powerful picture of a God whose loving concern was for every nation on earth. But these courageous voices were unheard by the majority. The increasing complexity of the political situation only served to obscure still further the gospel of right relationships. The voice of prophecy became silent. The experiment looked like being a failure.

A NEW VOICE

Then, in Roman-occupied Palestine, a new voice is heard. After twenty-nine years of silent involvement, a sermon is preached in a Nazareth synagogue. The scene ends in uproar. But already a new age has been inaugurated. This is the new and final chapter in the long story of man's exploration for right relationships. It is a chapter which is not yet closed.

The text of the sermon comes from the politician prophet (Isa. 61: 1, 2):

> The spirit of the Lord has been given to me,
> For He has anointed me.
> He has sent me to bring the good news to the poor,
> To proclaim liberty to captives
> And to the blind new sight,
> To set the downtrodden free,
> To proclaim the Lord's year of favour. (Lk. 4: 18ff.).

And St. Luke, writing with a vividness which suggests that he had the story from an eye-witness, tells how Jesus closed the book, and in an atmosphere of tense silence proclaims, 'This text is being fulfilled today even as you listen.'

The Spirit of the Lord is here pictured as the Spirit who creates right relationships. Poverty is a terrible divide down the middle of society. Prisoners are separated from their fellow-men by bars and stone walls. The blind are cut off by darkness from the world around them. The broken victims are those who, crushed in body and spirit, are paralysed in their attempt to go along with their fellow-men.

Here is the Good News of Freedom which Jesus came to inaugurate. For centuries the prophets had longed for the day when the barriers which divide man from his neighbour because they divide man from his God would come tumbling down. Here at last, in time and place in history, the Lord's year of favour is proclaimed.

PROCLAIMING THE GOOD NEWS

Later in this book we shall examine in more detail what all this means for the Christian Church. But here it should be asked whether the local Christian congregation sees that it is its duty to 'proclaim the year of the Lord's favour' in its own sphere of influence. Who are the blind in its own neighbourhood who need to be given sight? Who are the poor in need of good news? Who are the prisoners waiting to be released, and who are the broken victims waiting for their freedom? If the mission of the Church is to bear any relationship to the New Testament, these categories must be translated into the terms of today, and men and women in the local Christian congregations must learn how to take them seriously.

For it was precisely to be the instrument for the furtherance of the sermon preached in that Nazareth synagogue that Jesus called His Church into being. It was to be the new laboratory of right relationships, in succession to the community which God had called into being when Abraham left Ur of the Chaldees to work out in the Covenant the dual relationship between God and man, and man and his neighbour.

Increasingly, as the short earthly ministry of Jesus proceeds, the emphasis comes to be on the creation of the community which is called to discover unity in itself and a mission to bring wholeness to the world.

The Gospels give us plenty of evidence of the way Jesus set about training this group. There was the double element of withdrawal and dispersion. Whenever we read of the call of the Apostles, both these elements are there. 'He appointed twelve; they were to be his companions and to be sent out to preach' (Mk. 3: 14).

They were both to be His close companions, and to be sent out. Their training consisted of long hours of intimate fellowship with Him and with one another, followed by long missionary journeys in which they put His companionship to the test amongst all the divisions within man and within society. They had to bring to society the vision of a world in which the barriers which divide men would come tumbling down. The message of Jonah and Isaiah and the other prophets of right relationships could now be preached in its fullness.

But first they had to experience these right relationships within themselves. The message of unity which they were called to take to a disintegrated society had to come out of their own personal experience. And their own experience of right relationships could only be realized as they discovered the secret of right relationships with God. At first this puzzled them. Why cannot we see God? they would ask. And Jesus had to tell them that their experience of companionship with Him was the same thing as companionship with God. 'To have seen me is to have seen the Father' (Jn. 14: 9). But because their understanding of this was inadequate, the quality of their own community life remained fitful. More than once they seemed to have squabbled about who was the greatest.

St. Luke boldly records that they even fell to quarrelling immediately after the Last Supper when Jesus had, in a profoundly dramatic way, linked their fellowship with Him and with one another with His forthcoming sacrifice on the Cross. No sooner were the supper things cleared away than a 'dispute arose . . . which should be reckoned the greatest' (Lk. 22: 24). It is a tragic fact that, after two thousand years, the Holy Communion still proves to be the setting for jealous disputes among Christians.

Yet Jesus had already clearly stated that the test of discipleship would be found in the degree to which they had come to love one another. The quality of Christian community life matters far more than dogmatic orthodoxy or liturgical correctness. In the attempt to formulate the right statement of faith and order, it is all too easy to gain the whole world and to lose one's own soul. A Church which is not, above all else, a demonstration of the meaning of love within its own community life may be an interesting ecclesiastical phenomenon, but it is not the Body of Christ in the terms which the New Testament understands. And a Church which is not a demonstration of love within its own community life has no message for a divided world. It may have prestige, respectability, liturgical accuracy and theological correctness on its side. But, if it has not love, it is totally unable to be the instrument by which the message of the Nazareth sermon is brought in all its reality to the modern world.

This is why, when the crunch came, Jesus had to 'go it alone'. There was none other good enough.

The Cross shows how, at a white-hot point in history, God and man, and man and his neighbour, were perfectly brought into reconciliation. The search for right relationships in the long story of the Old Testament reached its fulfilment on a green hill outside a city wall.

THE WORDS FROM THE CROSS

The seven recorded utterances of Jesus from the Cross (Lk. 23: 34, 43; Jn. 19: 26; Matt. 27: 46; Jn. 19: 28, 30; Lk. 23: 46) provide the greatest commentary on this theme. Dietrich Bonhoeffer once described death as the last great festival on the road to freedom.[1] The words of Jesus from the Cross are the symbols of the triumphant progress by which God made real on the human stage the plan which the book of Genesis long ago had glimpsed; the vision that man could be completely at one with his neighbour and with his God. They are the cries of One who was in complete control of the situation. They are festival shouts, not gestures of despair. Because they reveal in a unique way the mission which Christ came to fulfil,

[1] *Letters and Papers from Prison.* S.C.M. Press, p. 176.

they point to the role of the Christian individually and of the Church corporately in each succeeding generation.

There is no part of human life for which these words do not have a profound meaning. They can be applied to the barriers between races and ideologies, to tensions in marriage and family life, to divisions in industry and in politics; in fact, to every part of the human scene where men are trying to discover the secret of living together. They speak both of the conditions and of the cost of perfect reconciliation. They also speak of the source of power without which all good intentions fall to the ground. And the event called the Resurrection, and the faith of those who believed in the Risen Christ, gave the guarantee that this drama of reconciliation, played out in time and space, was no delusion or wishful thinking.

THE LIVING LORD

It may be that we can never reconstruct for certain the events of the first Easter Day. But we only have to look at the life of the first Christian Church, as portrayed in the Acts of the Apostles and the Epistles, to see that in the years following the crucifixion, the Jesus of the Gospel stories is spoken of continually as One who is alive in great power in their midst. The first Christians did not face appalling odds in order to keep alive the memory of a good man now dead. They did the impossible only because they were spurred on by faith in the Living Lord.

Whatever did happen, it was in the small Christian community that the hopes of the Old Testament people found their fulfilment, and the right relationships which Christ came to bring saw their realization. The power of the Risen Christ was the power to break down barriers wherever His mighty acts were taken seriously and courageously translated into practical action.

To the first Christians the great guarantee that they were on the right track was to be found in the quality of relationships which existed within the Church. 'We have passed out of death and into life, and of this we can be sure because we love our brothers' (1 Jn. 3 : 14).

In the community which accepted the reconciling work of Christ, the barriers were beginning to be broken down already. The Church saw itself as a workshop of right relationships.

To St. Paul, surveying the developing life of the infant Christian Church, the great guarantee that God was at work in this new community was to be seen in the revolutionary quality of human relationships evident within it. Writing to the Galatians he says: 'All baptized in Christ, you have all clothed yourselves in Christ, and there are no more distinctions between Jew and Greek, slave and free, male and female, but all of you are one in Christ Jesus' (Gal. 3 : 28).

A similar list occurs in the letter to the Colossians, where again Paul affirms that, in the community of the baptized, men have put on 'a new self which will progress towards true knowledge the more it is renewed in the image of its creator; and in that image there is no room for distinction between Greek and Jew, between the circumcised or the uncircumcised, or between barbarian and Scythian, slave and freeman. There is only one Christ: he is everything and he is in everything' (Col. 3 : 11).

Notice that Paul is speaking not from theory but from experience. He does not say that these divisions ought not to exist. He says that in Christ they do not exist. In Christ, the divisions which are the commonplace of society are done away.

It is important to note that, in the passage from the letter to the Colossians, St. Paul appears to link these new relationships with the purpose of God in Creation that man should be made in His image. We have already seen how in the brilliant insights of the Genesis myths, the evidence that man has strayed from the purpose of God is founded on the fact of shattered relationships in the main areas of human life. Adam and Eve initiate the sex war. Cain and Abel bring murder to the factory floor. The arrogance of the city builders brings discrimination and racialism to political life. This was the situation which Paul (like ourselves) knew only too well. There was a sharp differentiation between the roles of men and women in society. There was an iron curtain down the middle of industrial life, dividing into sharp categories the freeman and the slave. The Jews practised a rigid code of racial segregation, only allowing integration for the strict necessities of commercial or political life. The Greek looked down at those who had not inherited the superb culture of Hellenism, and who (as the word 'barbarian' implies) could not even speak his lovely language. These were the accepted divisions of society. And, as is usual with accepted divisions, most people thought that they were part and parcel of God's will. The lessons of Genesis and the Book of Jonah had not yet been learned.

In its early days the Christian Church did not consciously set out to be a revolutionary movement. It found itself driven by a power it could hardly understand to press forward in its mission to break through the accepted barriers of the day. And the revolution in right relationships did not happen without much heart searching and internal strife. Here was the rock upon which the infant Church nearly foundered.

So the Christian Church began to glimpse the great truth that seen within the dimension of Christ's loving sacrifice, politics, race, industry and sex, all of which have become such dividing forces amongst men, could become the means of holy communion with God and with man. And Sunday by Sunday, in the gathering together for the Breaking of the Bread, the Church began to experience these tremendous truths within its own life.

And so Christians began to see that the mission of the

Church was to bring this new experience of right relationships in Christ to an ever-widening circle of people. This was the *raison d'être* of the Christian community: 'God in Christ was reconciling the world to Himself, not holding men's faults against them, and He has entrusted to us the news that they are reconciled' (2 Cor. 5: 19).

3

OUTLOOK ON MISSION

EMIL BRUNNER ONCE SAID that the Church existed for mission as fire exists for burning. By this, he meant that the only reason why the Church came into being was that it might share its knowledge of God with all mankind. Having itself been a laboratory of right relationships, it must then discover how to make these relationships relevant and active in the secular community.

The great vision of right relationships which the Bible brings to us is in tune with the deepest hopes and aspirations of men and women everywhere, and of every generation. The search for reconciliation in politics or race relationships, in the problems of sex or industry, in the factors which divide the generations and different cultural groups, can never be out of date. The Biblical evidence, as well as the best Christian experience of every generation, makes it abundantly clear that in so far as the Church is unable to speak to the modern world with relevance or with power, she is herself to blame. She has been entrusted with the ministry of reconciliation, and has failed to live up to that trust.

What, then, is the mission of the Church in the modern world, and how can she become fitted for it?

WORD AND DEED

The ministry of reconciliation is fulfilled both by the proclamation of the Good News (Evangelism) and by acts of service and reconciling love in a divided and suffering world. Mission is fulfilled by word and deed.

These two elements cannot be isolated from one another or treated in separation. Words without deeds can become empty and meaningless. Deeds without the proclamation of the Word may obscure the inner facts of the human situation, and result in superficial and partial remedies, rather than in a message of wholeness for man in his totality.

Yet the Church must beware of claiming to have an exclusive right to be the instrument of God's mission in the world. Through many different kinds of people and in many situations God has spoken in the past, and doubtless will continue to speak so in the future. When the Church is faithless and loses its 'sense of mission', it seems as though God is forced to seek other channels of communication. There are times (and perhaps the present is one of them) when God finds it easier to speak the Gospel of Reconciliation through the secular world than through the organized Church. Humanists and self-styled agnostics sometimes appear to be nearer the wavelength of Jesus Christ than the regular churchgoer, or those much absorbed in ecclesiastical affairs. Right relationships between men and women or young and old, are certainly worked out more fully in secular organizations than in the institutional Church where such divisions are supposed no longer to exist.

If God were able only to fulfil His mission through Christians, we would be in a sorry state. The fact that He often by-passes religious or ecclesiastical channels is one of the continual grounds for hope. Yet to say this is not to excuse the Church from her special mission in the world. It is only to shame her into pursuing it with greater faithfulness.

Nor, when we talk about the mission of the Church, must we speak too glibly about the task of the Church as 'bringing God to the world'. People sometimes talk about taking God into industry, or education, or whatever, as if He were a kind of commodity to be dumped on appropriate doorsteps. This is God's world, and He does not need the Church in order to be present in it.

One of the great discoveries which a deep sense of mission can bring is that in whatever situation we find ourselves, God is already there. Our task is never to bring God to people, but rather to open their eyes to the fact of His presence and activity all around them. This is why theology can only be understood within the context of the secular. For theology is the means by which we explain and explore the fact of God in the secular world around us. Mission is the making manifest of the unknown God in the midst.

Therefore, although Christians must not presume to say that they have exclusive rights to being the revealers of God at work in His own world, they can nevertheless dare to claim that they have a special calling to be the instruments of His mission. The failure and the faithlessness of the Church must not blind us to its particular and essential role within the purpose of God.

What is this role?

A STORY TO TELL

The Church has the task of proclamation. There is a story to tell: what God has done in history. At the heart of this proclamation is the revelation of Scripture. It is of the mission of the Church to cherish the Bible, to study it with honest scholarship, to preach it with integrity, and to encourage men and women to use it with devotion and intelligence. Although the old type of expository preaching (for which some people still yearn) is probably outdated and would be ineffective now, it must be confessed that there is little inspiration or exhilaration in the way in which the Bible is preached in many churches today. Few Christians are able to get the experience of effective corporate Bible study, and in spite of the good work of the Bible-Reading Fellowship, the International Bible-

Reading Association, and the Scripture Union, the few who use such schemes regularly tend to see Bible reading as a personal pious habit from which some comfort may be derived.

For the great majority of Christians, the Bible is a more or less closed book, only partially opened by readings (often inaudible or unintelligible) during the Sunday services. We need to discover ways of presenting the great and dramatic sweep of Scripture in such a way that people will press forward to hear the Word of God (Lk. 5: 1). We Christians say that it is our task to proclaim the mighty Acts of God revealed in Scripture, but the observer from the side might be excused if he came to the conclusion that we have ourselves become somewhat bored with the Bible. A certain kind of familiarity has already bred contempt.

The focus of our proclamation is Jesus Christ. The Church must proclaim not only the Christ of the Gospels, but the Christ of Christian experience. This means taking seriously the corporate testimony of the Christian Church all down the centuries, and the individual testimony of those who have known Christ as Master and Saviour. There is particular need to proclaim the evidence of the living Christ in the corporate and individual life of the Church of our own day. People hear Christians talking about the 'Living Christ', or 'Christ for Today', and they have good reason to ask what this is all about.

From Sunday School and day school days they have been used to seeing Christ represented as a figure of fairly distant history. He speaks, and is spoken to in an old-fashioned language. Even those who speak most loudly and eloquently about 'the power of Christ in their lives' seem to do so from the viewpoint of some strange distant world. The Christ they talk about is much more at home in a church or religious meeting than in a factory, a political party, a public house or a night-club.

The terrible quality of so much popular religious art,

music and poetry today presents a weary and anaemic picture of a sentimental 'has-been': the pale Galilean of the Swinburne poem whose only conquest was that the world had grown grey from his breath. This is the Christ of the popular Evangelistic Crusade, from whom a full-blooded man runs a mile for fear of catching this anti-quarian infection.

ESCAPE FROM A BLOODLESS CHRIST

I saw a good example of an attempt to escape from the bloodless Christ in a nativity play presented by a Liverpool girls' school. It began in a conventional way. The curtains parted, and there was Mary in blue, Joseph with a beard, a doll for the Baby, an assortment of shepherds and kings and angels with tissue paper wings. And in the background the school choir sang familiar carols to complete the picture. Then all the little angels held up letters which spelt HAPPY CHRISTMAS, and my heart sank. Was this to be just another corny Christmas play? I was soon proved to be wrong, for to my astonish-ment Mary and Joseph on the stage began to say exactly what I had been thinking.

'You make us look just like a Christmas card,' said Joseph to the angels. 'Plenty of people think of us as permanently fixed in a Nativity scene like this.'

Mary added, 'You make us seem like part of a fairy-tale world – useful to decorate the mantelpiece for a few days at Christmas, and then to be forgotten. Yet Jesus was born into a very real world on a cold night in a smelly stable. He must be out in the real world again, and Joseph and I must take him.'

And so, to the absolute horror of the shepherds, kings and angels, Mary and Joseph walk out of the picture leaving them dismayed. In the next scene we see them as a modern teenage couple in polo-necked sweaters and shiny macs. They are searching desperately for somewhere to have their baby, and find shelter at last in the basement of an inn, which a group of beatniks have been using as a folk club.

The point is obvious. Christians claim that Jesus Christ is a real figure of history. There is a significance in the fact that the Christian revelation can, to some extent at least, be tied down to time and place and date. Yet the mission of the Church is not primarily to proclaim a fact of history, even though this may be the starting point. It is not the Christ of 'once upon a time', but the Christ of today who must be proclaimed. Our mission is neither to give a history lesson, nor to hold out a carrot about 'pie in the sky when you die'. It is to proclaim a powerful way of life here and now. And that way of life has to do with Jesus Christ.

THE WHOLE OF LIFE

The proclamation is also about God at work in the world today. This is the particular task of prophecy. The prophet discerns the mercy of God in contemporary events in the secular world. He testifies to the fact that men and women are fellow workers with God, even when they do not recognize Him or claim to have any belief in Him. But the prophet must also testify to the judgment of God in contemporary events. Here he has to be ready to stand 'over and against' the world, and to say 'Thus says the Lord'.

All this means that the Christian mission is not just concerned with a part of life which might be labelled 'religion'. The Christian is concerned with the whole of life, seen within the perspective and context of God's revelation. Mission refuses to see a distinction between secular and sacred, or between religion and life. As Bishop Westcott was fond of saying, there is nothing secular except what is sinful. Mission is as much concerned with industrial, sexual or social relationships as it is with public worship or private prayer. Mission sees that the life of politics and Holy Communion are all of a piece, and that it is nonsense to say that one is more important than the other, or that one has genuine relevance without the other. So, in its mission to proclaim the mercy and judgment of God in the events of today, the Church must be seen to have a deep knowledge and concern for the world. Worldliness is a basic part of mission.

LEARNING THE LANGUAGE

When we talk about the role of the Church as proclamation, to whom do we refer? To the bishops and professional ministers of the Gospel? Those who are paid to preach have a special responsibility, and the whole Church is often judged on whether or not they do their job effectively. Yet the proclamation of the Gospel is the task of the whole Christian community. Every Christian is a missionary. In order to proclaim, the Church must enlist men and women in its missionary service. It must call them to share in God's task of peace-making in the world, and those who are so entrusted with the ministry of reconciliation must be given both training and rations for the job.

Training involves a serious study of the Word, and a serious study of the World. Rations are the resources for mission which God has given in the Church; sacrament, fellowship and the life of prayer. Without this training, men will not know what the message is with which they have been entrusted, nor will they understand the language in which they must address the world. Hendrik Kraemer once said that the first task of the missionary is to learn the language. However well the Christian has 'got the message' he will not be able to communicate it until he had been to language school.

The new sciences of psychology and sociology have much help to give to the Christian as he learns the language of his own mission field. He can also learn much

from the large number of people who are now professionally concerned with the mass media of communication.
Good television programmes and the highly efficient
mass circulation newspapers often make our attempts to
present the Gospel appear shoddy, amateur and ham-
fisted. It is easy to excuse ourselves by saying that these
people have money and resources available to them which
the Church cannot command. However true that may be,
it remains that in the art of communication, as in so much
else, the children of this world are 'more astute in dealing
with their own kind than are the children of light' (Lk.
16: 8).

RESOURCES

But neither the message nor the language are adequate
without the resources. To many devout Christians, the
place and meaning of prayer today raises many acute
problems. Much of the traditional teaching about the
devotional life given to laity in our churches is of little
help. In many theological colleges clergy are given training
in spiritual discipline which owes more to a distant monas
tic past than to the realities of the present day. Clergy,
who have been given very little help themselves, are at a
loss to know how to be of use to the people in their
congregations. Only now (and not before time) is serious
consideration being given to a lay spirituality which is not
a pallid imitation of what the clergy are supposed to do,
but the spiritual equipment which the layman needs for
his task of mission in the modern world.

At the heart of the mission of the Church lies its worship.
It is in worship that we celebrate God's call to share in
His mission. We do this in two ways: it is a response to the
God who acts, and it is a proclamation, through corporate
words and actions, of the message of reconciliation.

We respond to the God who acts by adoration, praise and
thanksgiving, intercession and petition. In the reading
and proclamation of the Word and in the setting forth of

the Sacrament of the Lord's Supper, we discover our two-fold vocation to come together in unity, and to be dispersed in the world in mission. In the past we have sometimes spoken of 'mission services'. But all worship is part of the mission of the Church because it is the action of the Christian community in the world as it responds to the God who speaks, acts and sends.

We shall be examining later certain implications for a community which dares to claim to follow the 'Man for others'. But it is clear that a Church which exists for others must often be prepared to lose its identity in order to be in a position to serve. This is just what most ecclesiastical organizations find so difficult to do. The less certain the Church is about its role in the community, the more anxious it is to take every opportunity to draw attention to itself. The Church further hinders its own task of mission if its activities appear to be a last ditch attempt to salvage a dying institution. It quickly becomes obsessed with its own survival. Yet if we take the New Testament at all seriously, it always has to be asked whether part of the mission of the Church may not be to be prepared to lose its identity and die. Does such a text as 'Unless a wheat grain falls on the ground and dies' (Jn. 12: 24) apply only to the individual? May it not have meaning for the institutional Church as well? Is not part of our ineffectiveness due to an anxiety to cling on to existing structures for dear life? Mission may appear to be nothing more than an attempt to inject new life into old structures which should long ago have been discarded. If death and resurrection are to be part of the pattern of Church life too, we are certainly doomed if mission becomes only a thinly disguised ecclesiastical salvage operation.

ESTABLISHMENT OUT

All this means that the renewal of the Church is a basic part of its mission. Particularly it must be questioned how much the present static institutionalism of the Church actually hinders its mission. People are no longer interested in being caught up into a structure which looks as though it is irrelevant to the present age.

In Great Britain today, all denominations have become part of what is loosely called the Establishment. They take their place among those slow-moving institutions of society which seem bent on preserving the *status quo* at a time of change. To belong to this institution and to conform to its cultural and moral pattern is to become imprisoned in a system which, however well intentioned, appears to have very little to do with the revolutionary Gospel of the New Testament. It is because they see the dangers of an institutionalism which seems to conflict with the 'glorious liberty of the children of God' (Rom. 8: 21, A.V.) that more and more people are becoming attracted to movements which try to keep the Christian Faith alive, but are ready to discard the Church. The non-Church movement cannot merely be dismissed as the crazy idea of *avant-garde* discontents, or theological students who are afraid of the traditional disciplines of the Christian ministry. It grows out of renewed concern for the Christian mission. It is a genuine (though possibly misplaced) attempt to free the Church from its ecclesiastical bondage in order to enable it to fulfil its proper evangelistic task.

Within the Churches themselves, growing doubts about the effectiveness of the institution give rise to feverish internal activity. Many of them are going through hectic periods of domestic reconstruction. Commissions and committees are set up on every conceivable subject: liturgical reform, structural reform, unity discussions, and much else. But busy Churches should ask themselves seriously how much all this activity helps to equip them for more effective mission, and how much it is the familiar process of moving the furniture about when it is the whole house which has caught fire. Internal activity can become a substitute for both mission and genuine renewal.

ORGANIZE FOR MISSION

How can the local church become organized for mission? How can it become conscious of itself as the servant of the community, entrusted with the message of reconciliation?

The Church in Britain is still organized largely on a parochial or congregational basis. Even when (as in the Church of England) there is a parochial system, the concept of over-all pastoral responsibility for a large area becomes a pious hope rather than a reality. When the vicar, with or without the help of one or two curates, is given the cure of souls in a parish of ten or twenty thousand people, this 'cure' can be nothing but a hit-and-miss affair. In fact, all church systems today tend increasingly to become 'congregational'. But what happens under such circumstances to the concept of the Church as the servant to the whole community, when it appears to be a service organization for a limited (and diminishing number) of adherents?

To put it another way, what relationship does a local congregation bear to the facts of life of its own district? Furthermore, does the catchment area of a church correspond with any sociological reality? In towns, parish boundaries often appear to be arbitrary, and the siting of churches haphazard. In villages, pluralities and widespread circuits are organized more often for staffing convenience than for any relationship to the community. And, more profoundly, it has to be asked, as the Church surveys her missionary task in Britain today, whether the local congregation ('parochial' or 'gathered') has very much relevance to the community in which it operates.

People today inhabit many different 'worlds' simultaneously. Family, neighbourhood, work, political and cultural interests, means of transport and communication, all play their part in determining these 'worlds'. Certainly the parish, based on some kind of territorial unit, can no longer go on claiming to be the whole Church in miniature. Less and less are people caught up in the concerns of their immediate geographical neighbourhood. They find their interests across a wide area of a city or district. Their immediate neighbourhood only supplies a small part of their needs. The 'parish pump' has an insignificant part in their lives.

To restrict the organized Christian community to the local neighbourhood group will immediately suggest that the Church is a local spare-time activity, of comparatively trivial significance, and of occasional use, like the village stores or the local public house. The real centres of interest, whether industrial, political, commercial, cultural, social, are not reflected in this immediate neighbourhood, and are therefore nothing to do with the Church.

This makes it imperative that the Church develops types of ministry independent of and supplementary to the ministry in the local congregation. We have long been accustomed to this in the armed forces, the prison service, hospitals and schools. These have been justified as legitimate extensions of the parochial ministry. An army unit, a battleship, a prison, or a hospital are, after all, kinds of parish. As such, the Church has been happy to accept these ministries. Ministries in other fields, such as youth work and industry, are becoming part of the pattern.

Yet the majority of clergy working in local congregations view such ministries with a degree of suspicion. Anglicans tend to dismiss those of their fellows who work in specialized ministries as 'not having an altar', and Free Church ministers are inclined to ask their specialist brethren when they will be returning into 'the working ministry'. A rural dean (who ought to have known better) said of a very hard-working diocesan youth organizer, 'He's a good man. Pity he is not in a parish.' It really did not occur to the rural dean that the youth chaplain, working closely with the local authority youth service, the voluntary organizations, and *ad hoc* groups of boys and girls in folk clubs and the like, was probably doing a far more effective task of mission than any of the parochial clergy in his deanery.

EXPERIMENTS IN MINISTRY

At the moment it is the parochial clergy who consider themselves to be the mainstay of the Church. The specialists are strange 'way-out' ministers of doubtful value. The myth that the local congregational unit, or the parochial 'cure of souls', must be the normal strategy for mission will die hard; but it will have to die. Of course there will be a place for the local parish ministry, just as medicine will always require the general practitioner. But if the Church is to be an effective instrument for the ministry of reconciliation, there will have to be a bold exploration of the nature and function of priesthood in all areas of life where human relations are significant and the welfare and happiness of mankind promoted. The social services, the world of art and culture, the places of political decision, the great centres of technology and science, the formative points in the world of mental and physical health, the field of entertainment and mass communication: these all transcend the local neighbourhood, and require a priestly and prophetic ministry where the Church can both discern the voice of God speaking through the secular, and declare the Word of God speaking to the secular. Such specialist and experimental ministries, if they are to have the finance and the training they require, must have at least equal status in the Church with the parochial ministry.

This does not absolve the local congregation from its task of witnessing to the Gospel in its own locality. Nor do the foregoing paragraphs about the need for experimental specialist ministries mean to imply that the clergy are the main factors in the mission of the Church. It is the task of the whole Church to be missionary; and in the Church the laity far outnumber the clergy.

How can the laity in the local congregation equip themselves for mission in their own locality? They must learn to see that the local Church is an instrument designed to proclaim reconciliation in the world. It is not an end in itself.

4

OUTLOOK ON MINISTRY

As EVERY NEW MINISTER knows when visiting the older stalwarts of the congregation, there is a widespread belief that 'the Church is not what it was in our young day'. Pictures of former ministers on the vestry walls, and of choir groups or Boys' Brigade Companies on the pianos in the homes of the faithful, promulgate the myth that the great days of the local congregation lay in the past, and that this former glory must at all costs be recaptured. There is a dominant element of conservatism in the local congregation. The familiar hymn tunes, the time-honoured organizations, the older ways of doing things must be clung to for dear life's sake. Even minor changes are made in the teeth of fierce opposition. The new minister will go carefully for fear of alienating the more powerful members of his flock. He feels that, if he upsets people with innovations, he will no longer have the contact with them which his pastoral office demands. That is why, in the Church of England, radical curates tend to become less radical as vicars. And fire-brand vicars become the pillars of conservative respectability when elevated to the episcopal bench! Such high store is placed on pastoral responsibility that almost any price seems worth paying to keep the lines of communication intact. This is good sense. Yet the price may sometimes be a little too high.

It is a platitude to say that in both urban and rural areas the pattern of life is changing rapidly. It is equally obvious that this changing pattern requires that all church structures must be seen as temporary and flexible. The structure of the local Church designed to meet the needs of one century tends to be preserved in a more or less pickled state into the next. The result is a paralysis which makes progress slow and painful. Somehow or another, local Churches must be rescued from the paralysis of institutionalism. They must free themselves from their sense of established security, and discover once again what it means to be a pilgrim people of God. They must 'learn to travel light', and that to be pilgrims they must 'discard much precious ecclesiastical baggage'.[1] They must stop thinking of themselves as settled institutions or clubs for the religious, and re-discover what it means to be a mission station in territory which has always to be charted afresh.

THE NEED TO BE OUTWARD LOOKING

This can only happen if the members of local congregations learn afresh the great Biblical insights of the call of God to His people to be a 'kingdom of priests' and to 'go into all the world to preach the Gospel'. The local Church must reorientate its vision in order to be primarily outward looking on the world rather than inward looking on itself. It must, in the Geneva jargon, learn to be 'go-structured' rather than 'come-structured'.

So it must have its eyes wide open to what is going on in its own locality, keeping the life of the local community under constant survey. This is difficult because few clergy, or church laity, have any training in sociology. Yet, without this constant appraisal, the local Church cannot fulfil the first task of the missionary and 'learn the language'. It will continue to answer questions which nobody is asking in a language which nobody can understand. Too often, discussion on mission still begins by asking

[1] Report of the Third World Conference on Faith and Order, Lund, 1952 (Faith and Order Commission, World Council of Churches), p. 10.

D

how the local community can be 'brought in'. But the
first question must be about the real situation of the local
community, and only then to ask about the place of the
local Church within it.

What evidence is there that those who go to church are
compelled to take the local community more seriously
than those who stay away? Do the columns of the parish
magazine or the information on the notice-board demonstrate that the church is not only interested in itself and
in its own affairs? Examine the programme of talks
given to the Mothers' Union or Sisterhood, to the Men's
Club, Young Wives or Youth Fellowship. It is tragic
how often the syllabus is taken up with trivia. Slides taken
by the vicar when he went to Oberammergau twenty
years ago, or a talk by some local lady on flowers and
birds in the Old Testament! Nobody suggests that all
church organizations should run university extension
lectures, but there ought to be clear evidence that those
who call themselves Christians have a heightened aware-
ness of the world around them, because they know that it
is God's world and it is the theatre within which He has
chosen to work out the drama of redemption. Every
local Church must ask itself continuously how it can be
of direct service to the neighbourhood it seeks to serve. Are
there ways in which its premises can be offered for such
uses as an open youth centre, an ante-natal clinic, an
old people's welfare centre and the like? The more
church buildings can be used for non-ecclesiastical
activities, the easier it will be for people to believe that
the church is a genuine caring community, and not a
self-perpetuating institution.

BETTER USE OF MAN-POWER

Furthermore, the call to service means the willingness to
make people (and not just buildings) available for work
outside the Church, even if this sometimes depletes the

man-power of the Church's own activities. In any event, a careful scrutiny needs to be made of Church organizations to ask whether they are achieving anything in proportion to the time and energy involved, or whether they are tying up man-power urgently needed elsewhere. The Church would discover the meaning of mission more readily if there were a greater willingness to examine ruthlessly its priorities in terms of time, money and personnel in the congregation.

Many so-called secular organizations are doing the reconciling work of mission, even when they shun using religious or Biblical language to describe their work. Who can deny that those concerned with marriage guidance, alcoholics anonymous, community service volunteers, youth club leadership, old people's welfare and the like, are sharing with the Church in God's mission of service and reconciliation? The parable of the sheep and the goats continually reminds us of this. 'In so far as you did this to one of the least of these brothers of mine, you did it to me' (Matt. 25: 40). Often these organizations are in desperate need of more workers. Many of those who work with them are already members of local congregations. Increasingly, areas of social work which the Church pioneered in the past are now rightly the concern of statutory authorities, but the need for voluntary helpers working with the statutory services remains. Yet the pioneer church-centred organizations are often reluctant to let go of their own vested interests in the social work field, and to take a share in the ministry of a secular body; and there is still too much evidence of churches being unwilling to release their lay helpers to work in these secular organizations.

In the spring of 1969, the Board for Social Responsibility of the Church of England presented to the Church Assembly a Report entitled *The Church and the Social Services*.[1] It was able to report that:

[1] Church Information Office, 1969, p. 23.

Churches are getting together to meet local needs. There are projects for visiting the elderly, the handicapped and the lonely, variously described as 'Fish', or 'Good Neighbour', or 'Street Warden' schemes. There are housing projects, play centre projects, community centre projects. Sometimes the inspiration for these comes from one of the clergy, sometimes from a Council of Churches, sometimes from a statutory social work administrator and so forth.

Yet, on the debit side, it had to be admitted that:

It was harder to come by evidence that clergy with their congregations were willing to co-operate in the activities of the statutory services in their locality, as for example ensuring that the staff and residents of local authority establishments such as old people's homes, were welcomed into the life of the local Christian community. Many individual Christians are involved in social service but frequently feel that they are inadequately backed up by the clergy and their congregations as a whole. There is also the feeling that members of Christian congregations so involved are few in number and that clergy and people in their congregations should be encouraging their members to take a more lively and informed part in the social services.[1]

The Seebohm Report on the Social Services[2] made it clear that the whole community has the responsibility of bearing the burdens of all, which Scripture describes as 'fulfilling the law of Christ'. There is no doubt that the welfare state provides the Christian Church with opportunities for service to the community as great as at any time in history. This is part of the evangelistic task, if only the Church has the vision and humility to pursue it in a rapidly changing social welfare situation.

But the main area of Christian service is in the sphere of daily work. Work is no less service to the community because it is rewarded with a salary cheque, yet the idea dies hard that Christianity is a leisure-time activity and

[1] op. cit., p. 24.
[2] The Seebohm Report. Report of the Committee on Local Authorities and Allied Personal Social Services. H.M.S.O., 1968.

Christian service is that which is given in spare time. If the local Church had a broader concept of the nature of mission it would be devoting more of its thought and time to discovering how Christian men and women could be helped to relate the Gospel of Jesus Christ to their daily work. Christian service would be seen to be relevant to problems of management, trades unionism, productivity, staff training and appointments, and all the complexities of group relationships in the working world.

CLERGY AND LAITY

This reorientation of the Church towards the world necessitates a new look at the role of the clergy, and their relationship with the laity. Too often, the clergy have considered themselves the leaders in the local Church and the laity as their loyal supporters. Many of the laity have been glad to follow the lead of the clergy, but the mission of the Church, in the sense in which we have been discussing it, makes something like the reverse order nearer the truth. The laity are in the front line because they are involved in the world's work. They are the leaders of the Christian advance. The clergy are called to play a humbler, though necessary, part as the backroom boys providing ammunition for those battling on the frontiers. The New English Bible (but not the Authorized Version) translation of Ephesians, chapter 4, makes this clear. The ministry (pastors, evangelists, prophets and teachers) exist to 'equip God's people for work in His service'.

This new understanding of ministry, in which the clergy are seen to be sharing with the laity in the mission of the Church, is certainly Biblical, and yet comes as something of a shock to those ordained ministers who had become used to thinking of themselves as placed on the pedestal of leadership. Clergy have sometimes taken a 'not in front of the children' attitude towards the laity. They have preferred not to share with them the ups and downs of modern theological controversy. To some, the great sin of *Honest to God*[1] was that it was published in an inexpensive paper edition, and therefore easily accessible. It is better to encourage laymen to concern themselves with practical issues, such as the heating apparatus or the envelope scheme, and leave the theology to the professionals! More particularly, many of the clergy have been worried lest their people might become over-exposed to the ecumenical movement. They might get dangerous ideas, or start breaking the rules (constructed by clergymen) as to who may share communion with whom, and under what circumstances. At one time, young people of one denomination were only allowed to fraternize with their contemporaries in another denomination after the most thorough indoctrination into 'what our Church teaches'.

That these fears and attitudes are still with us was instanced when the British Council of Churches inaugurated a great national campaign for ecumenical group work in the spring of 1966. It was called The People Next Door Campaign, and the official report discloses considerable unease from professional ministers because the scheme encouraged lay leadership. One group commented:

> We met with non-interest and even active hostility from some ministers which meant that a rather modest attempt was all we could manage.[2]

Another area commented:

> Numbers seemed to depend entirely on the clergy or minister's push. The fact that many did push and give tremendous impetus to P.N.D. shows that the complaint by others that they did not know enough (or anything) about P.N.D. covers a considerable blockage. The blockage is made up of (a) being unable to cope with anything new;

[1] John A. T. Robinson, S.C.M. Press, 1963.
[2] *Agenda for the Churches*. A Report on The People Next Door Campaign, S.C.M. Press, 1968, p. 12.

(b) fear of losing effective control of their Church; (c) insularity; (d) dislike of courses imposed from outside.[1]

The report makes it clear that this attitude of the clergy and ministers in many areas profoundly disturbed their lay members. It led to some very forthright observations from different parts of the country:

> The chief stumbling block to unity is the clergy and ministers. All clergy ought to attend courses of Christian unity run by laymen.
>
> The clergy gave birth to us as a body, and it is not known whether they wish us to continue as a body – or whether they think that they have created a monster and we should now be exterminated.
>
> We feel that the barrier between minister and laity is greater than that between the denominations.

And one group in militant mood exclaimed:

> You parsons had better watch out – you may find the laity demanding unity if you let us get together like this.[2]

This explosion in the largely Protestant world had its counterpart a couple of years later, after the publication of the Papal Encyclical, *Humanae Vitae*, which produced a lay revolt that on any reckoning must be counted of greater importance for the future of the Church than the Papal words themselves.

> The kindest comment one can make about the statement (wrote one Catholic layman) is that it arises from ignorance of the marital situation. The alternative would be a charge of hypocrisy. Neither is a qualification for the making of authoritarian pronouncements.[3]

And another writer concluded a long letter on the Pill with the words:

> I hope that as many of my fellow Catholic laymen as possible will not only ignore the ban, but make their

[1] *op. cit.*, p. 12.
[2] *op. cit.*, p. 22.
[3] *New Christian*, Aug. 8, 1968.

protests loud and clear to their bishops, their clergy, and their fellow lay Christians. The ban must be rejected both as an affront to our consciences and as a scandal to our fellows.[1]

It was instructive to notice how the statements made by the more progressive members of the Roman Catholic hierarchy in Britain following the post-encyclical explosion showed a real sensitivity to lay opinion, and a genuine desire to take it seriously.

The reaction to The People Next Door Campaign and the Pope's birth control pronouncement are two major straws in the wind which the Church of the future will have increasingly to take seriously. Clergy and laity must learn to 'come clean' with each other. The old play-acting and stock attitudes on both sides must give way to a frank and open co-operation in which their complementary roles are allowed to create an effective and genuine partnership. This is a major priority if the Church is to move forward with a relevant mission for the world of tomorrow. It is difficult for the Church to commend a Gospel of Reconciliation to a divided world if, at the heart of the Christian community, clergy and laity are at sixes and sevens, engaged in a perpetual demarcation dispute.

By the same token, there are other divisions in the local congregation which have to be examined if the Church is to be ready for mission. The whole Bible picture of the People of God shows that they are called to exhibit in themselves the spirit of reconciliation and peace. 'How these Christians love one another' was not first said with the tongue in the cheek. It was a spontaneous exclamation of the evident sense of community to be seen amongst the followers of Christ. We think, rightly enough, of ecumenism as the search for unity amongst divided Churches. But no less important is the search for unity in divided congregations. There, too, in the local Church, the followers of Christ must be one if the world is to believe.

[1] *New Christian*, Aug. 8, 1968.

SEX BARRIERS

There is the division between men and women. In a world in which the respective relationship of the sexes has changed rapidly, the Christian Church often seems to have lagged behind. The World Council of Churches has done some valuable work in its study on the co-operation between men and women both in church and in society. Some Churches have made considerable headway in the admission of women to the ministry, and to responsible positions in the life of the Christian community. But in many Churches the progress is distressingly slow.

Just as there are more women voters than men and fewer women representatives than men, so in the Church there are more women in the congregation than men, and more men than women office holders. An infinitesimal number of women are called to the levels where decisions are made, thinking done, and policy formed in commissions and synods.

The Vatican Council and the Lambeth Conference were both all-male affairs. Even in the Fourth Assembly of the World Council of Churches women were in a tiny minority. Onlookers might be excused for thinking that the Church was an organization for women run by men. The Church which claims that in its fellowship there 'is neither male nor female' gives the Holy Spirit very little chance to show the world what reconciliation in the sexual sphere is all about.

The section on 'Renewal in Ministry' in the Lambeth Conference which met under the chairmanship of the Archbishop of York, stated clearly that it:

> saw no conclusive theological reason for withholding Ordination to the priesthood from women as such.[1]

But when the report was presented to the whole synod of Bishops, the statement was watered down to placate the

[1] Lambeth Conference 1968, Report and Resolutions, S.P.C.K., p. 106.

conservative element. The considered mind of the Anglican Episcopacy now appears to be that:

> the theological arguments as at present presented for and against the ordination of women to the priesthood are inconclusive.[1]

Although the section at the Lambeth Conference which specifically dealt with this topic believed that there was no conclusive theological reason against the ordination of women, they saw what they called cultural considerations which they thought had to be taken very seriously.

> Hesitations in personal attitudes to the ordination of women are often related to cultural factors. The renewal of the Church in ministry must be achieved in a variety of cultural settings and environments, which differ from continent to continent, and may confront the Church with different cultural patterns within a single country. These will require careful study as we move to make possible the ordination of women within our communion. In countries and continents where women have already won acceptance as doctors and lawyers, and in business, politics and education, their acceptance as ordained ministers of Word and Sacrament may well prove easier than in areas where tradition and custom still confine most women to the home. The Church should take appropriate steps to educate its members to think constructively about the issues.[2]

Of course there is some truth in this. Yet it is a sad admission. Not only because there are no very clear signs that even in those countries where 'women have won acceptance as doctors, lawyers, etc.', does the Anglican Church appear to be any more ready to ordain women than elsewhere. But also because the Church, far from exercising a prophetic role in the community, must wait until medicine, the law, commerce, politics and education have blazed the trail before herself daring to demonstrate

[1] *op. cit.*, p. 39.
[2] *op. cit.*, p. 107.

right relationships between the sexes in her professional ministry. Like the Duke of Plaza Toro, she leads her regiment from behind. No wonder more and more people find her less and less exciting!

EQUAL MINISTRY

If the Church survives for long into the future it is inconceivable that an equal ministry of men and women will not in time become accepted as normal and right. People will marvel that the Church was once, and for so long, a stronghold of sex prejudice. But, long before women are admitted into the ordained ministry, a more sane attitude to the relationship of men and women must prevail both in the central government of the Church and in the life of the local congregation. At present women have practically no influence on policy making in most Churches. True, they are beginning to be represented on the central bodies of many of the Churches. But in the places where policy is really determined they are conspicuous by their absence. In the Church of England, the Convocations (unlike their temporal counterparts at Westminster) are all-male assemblies. In how many dioceses are women part of the bishop's staff meeting? There are today some noteworthy women leaders in the Church, but their names come all too easily to mind precisely because they are the exceptions which prove the rule.

What steps can be taken to right this lack of balance in the life of the Church? First, everything must be done to improve the status of full-time deaconesses and women workers. At present, the most experienced women workers or church sisters are given less responsibility (and usually less money) than a young curate straight from theological college. The medical and teaching professions would not stand for this. Furthermore, it is often assumed that the woman worker's job is to deal with women and children. In the sphere of social work it is often found that women are best suited to deal with men. Women doctors do not only treat female patients. Women judges do not only sentence women criminals. Part of the blame for this false attitude must rest on the clergy themselves. The only way to get this straight is to train men and women for their ministry together. More and more colleges for the training of teachers now cater for both sexes. Has not the time come for men and women to have their basic theological and pastoral training together? This is happening in some Free Church theological colleges, but it should become the normal pattern everywhere.

Turning to the local Church and its organizations, there is also much that can be done. Women have, of course, long been elected to parochial church councils and their equivalent in other Churches, but too often they are separated into social committees to become stall-holders and tea-makers while the men get on with what they con-sider to be the real business of running the Church. Can we not sometimes still detect on parochial church councils a survival of the Victorian myth that the man looks after the real business of the household and that the wife should not 'worry her pretty little head' about such things. How much does the local Church make serious use of the experience of life which many women in the congregation have gained as teachers, doctors, nurses, social workers, administrators and much else? Tea-making and even stall-holding may be necessary to parish life, but to confine women to such comparatively trivial jobs is to ignore the fact that we are living in the twentieth century.

Perhaps wrong attitudes are also encouraged by the perpetuation of single-sex organizations as a normal part of parish life. Fifty years ago our teenagers were put into separate societies for boys and girls. Today we recognize that the mixed group is the normal meeting-place for the adolescent. Nor do we any longer put men on one side of the church and women on the other! Yet in many local Churches the only organizations for adults are still the

Mothers' Union and the Men's Society. The occasional joint meeting is considered exceptional and even daring! Ought not the normal meeting of adults in the congregation be for men and women together? Should they not only meet in single-sex groups to fulfil specific jobs which are better done in this way?

We need an honest and critical examination of the relationship of men and women in the Church. Much that we take for granted in our ecclesiastical life has nothing whatever to do with basic Christianity. We are often frightened to liberate ourselves from the conventions of the past. As we look at the new relationship of men and women in secular society, it is difficult to resist the thought that God may find it easier to work there than within the Church itself. Certainly a Church which proclaims that in Christ there is neither male nor female can have little to say to the world of the future so long as it takes its stereotypes from the social attitudes of a past age. A Church which fails to come to grips with the question of right relationships between the sexes in its own life is ill-equipped to be entrusted with the message of reconciliation in a world which seems to be grappling with such questions with greater success.

OTHER DIVISIONS AND CONFLICTS

Other divisions in the local Church are between young and old; between Church officials, choir members and the ordinary congregation; between the regular members and the occasional visitor. And there is sometimes a real conflict of loyalties between specific organizations in the Church and the well-being of the whole congregation. At every point there must be regular appraisal of the situation and an attempt to deal honestly with the points of tension. A house divided against itself cannot stand, nor can it be a worthy instrument in God's mission of reconciliation.

It follows that the local Church is further crippled in

its task of mission when the outsider sees a number of self-centred religious organizations at best ignoring one another, and at worst in apparent competition. The development of local Councils of Churches has been one of the most important factors in the life of the post-war Church in Britain, and the involvement of the Roman Catholic Church in these councils in the last year or two has added immensely to their significance. Yet the several Churches in a locality can still send official representatives (usually one minister and two laymen) to a local Council of Churches meeting without their congregations becoming very much involved with one another.

PROGRESS TOWARDS UNITY

It is, once again, when small groups of laity get together across the denominational barriers that the big discoveries begin to be made. The People Next Door Campaign illustrated this again and again. One group reported that when:

> the initial sense of bewilderment that our fellow Christians in other denominations do not have horns and tails has worn off, we are left with several misconceptions less and many new friendships more.[1]

This is the necessary beginning; when Christians stop thinking of their fellow Christians in other denominations as 'them', and begin to see them as 'us'. But it has to go deeper.

> There is amongst most progressives much impatience, intolerance and possibly lack of understanding at the apparent slow progress in removing barriers at parish level between the various denominations. The course raised hopes that lay people will take matters into their own hands and speedily do something really effective.

[1] *Agenda for the Churches*, p. 22.

There is strong reason to believe, and to hope, that the main incentive towards radical and adventurous acts of unity, particularly at the local level, will come from the laity as they meet together to survey their common task as laymen in their mission in the community within which they live. It would be a tragedy if the lowest common denominator decisions of central bodies, often taken in a clinical and academic atmosphere, prevented the laity in the local Church from making the bold and dangerous experiments in joint mission and Christian community which the present situation and the eternal task of the Church demands.

5

OUTLOOK ON EVANGELISM

WE HAVE BEEN DISCUSSING in general the role of the Church as a community entrusted with mission, and the renewal which is essential if the instrument is to do its job in the modern world. What is the place of evangelism in all this?

Evangelism is that part of the mission of the Church in which the Gospel is announced as a fact to be believed and a gift to be accepted. This gift is offered through the spoken word; it is accepted in the mind and heart of the hearer.

The Church's task within the mission of God is wider than evangelism. Everything that manifests God's purpose for His world or fulfils that purpose is relevant to the task of making Christians. An act of service can make the Good News explicit to someone for whom words will never bring home the truth. Evangelism is not to be set over against service. Both can equally serve God's missionary purpose of redemption and reconciliation, and the bringing to men and women of that life which is Christ's gift to them. Yet many people are sceptical of a mission which seems to stop short of the call to commitment to Christ. We cannot be content with the creation of a vague and diffuse influence of good-will. The Good News of Christ must be boldly preached to men. It is for them to choose whether they accept or whether they reject it.

What is the responsibility of the local Church as a centre of 'direct evangelism'? Both clergy and laity need to examine together carefully and critically whether the fullest opportunities are being taken.

THE SPOKEN WORD

What about sermons? It is often said that the day of the sermon is over. Yet in almost every church in the land two sermons are delivered every Sunday. The sum total of words uttered from pulpits each year is awe-inspiring. Probably neither clergy nor laity take sermons as seriously as once they did. There are many reasons for this. The tricks of oratory which characterized many of the great preachers of the past would make little impact on hearers today. If they came back to our pulpits now, it would be like seeing an old film which had been a great success in its own day, but which, when repeated thirty or forty years later, seems curiously jaded and unconvincing.

The personality cult of the preacher does not have the same drawing power as once it did, though evangelical churches in particular still draw crowds to a few key 'personality pulpits'. But, by and large, people speak much less often than once they did of 'going to hear Mr. Blank' when referring to the act of divine worship! This is certainly a gain.

This change of attitude has something to do with the better standard of education in the congregation, and (perhaps) the lower standard of education in the pulpit. It is certainly linked with the highly professional techniques of communication with which we have become familiar through radio and television. Much public preaching, and the acts of worship which surround it, are sometimes less carefully prepared than the television weather forecast! For this reason, the average congregation has come to expect very little from sermons. The great preachers of the past expected to be met half-way by their hearers, in much the same way as a great actor or television comedian raises the hopes of the audience even before the performance has begun. In a few churches where people come deliberately to hear the star preachers

E

week by week, you can detect a starry-eyed look of hope and admiration in the eyes of the fans in the congregation as the great man ascends the pulpit steps.

It would be foolish to deny that this kind of top-billing preaching is without value altogether. Many ardent Christians owe their first real understanding of the Gospel to such men. But it is equally foolish to believe that this can any more be expected to be the normal method of communication in the local church. In fact, the sermons of many of the most popular evangelical preachers (including Billy Graham) which make a great initial impact on the susceptible hearer, are found on further analysis to have very little content to them.

For most Christians trying to make sense of their faith in the rough and tumble of the modern world sermons provide an insufficient diet. Yet in most congregations preaching has become an essential part of every act of worship. For many people, it is not a 'proper service' unless there is a sermon. This means that most clergy have to preach far too often. It is asking too much of most men to produce two sermons a Sunday for fifty-two weeks in the year. This is why the average parson can be found sitting in his study towards the end of the week, anxiously looking up the Epistle or Gospel or set Lections for the coming Sunday in the desperate hope that they will give him a clue on 'what to preach about'.

Regular speakers on television programmes such as 'Panorama' or 'Twenty-four Hours' have a team of experts and research workers behind them to help with their contributions. The parson often feels himself very much alone. It is his job to find something to say two or three times a week, with no resources apart from his experience and a meagre library. Perhaps the standard of preaching in the local church would be improved if those who have to preach regularly also learned to rely on research teams, as the television people do. But what does this mean?

DYNAMIC BIBLE

It means, first and foremost, that the man who preaches from the Bible must continue to gain exhilaration from his study of the Word of God. It is not enough to look up the commentaries simply to elucidate next Sunday's text. Most people (including the clergy) can only get really excited about the Bible when they have the opportunity of studying it with other people in a small group. Ruridecanal chapters and ministers' fraternals should spend a good deal more time in reading the Word of God together than they do in discussing wedding fees or cemetery duties.

Even these groups may be too big for effective corporate Bible study. It is when a few people gather round the fire in someone's house in order to discover together what God has to say to them in Scripture that Bible study becomes a dynamic and inspiring experience. It is here that discoveries about God are made which will command close attention when drawn on later from the pulpit in church. It sounds too simple to suggest that the standard of preaching today is generally low because of the clergy's lack of experience of regular and dynamic Bible study. But this is probably near the truth. So the preacher's research team is first to be found in joint study with his fellow preachers.

His other and equally important researchers are the laity to whom he preaches. To be a missionary to them, he must 'learn their language'. There are constant complaints from men and women in the pews that their ministers 'talk above their heads'. It is difficult to believe that this really means that the sermons are so intellectual that they cannot be understood except by hearers of equal brainpower! What lies behind so many of these complaints is the fact that the words uttered in the pulpit just fail to connect with the everyday experience of the hearers.

To remedy this requires something more than the

inclusion of a few topical or homely illustrations. It means being true to the Gospel of the Word which became flesh and dwelt among men. Jesus did not just use illustrations from everyday life to drive home His points. He conveyed the very stuff of the Gospel from within the experience of the secular. He was the least 'churchy' of preachers. He was the lay-preacher *par excellence*. And the common people heard Him gladly, and knew that He lived in their world, was tempted in all ways as they were, and spoke their own language. This is why the preacher today can only proclaim the Gospel to his flock with any meaning if he is in the closest possible touch with them. This means getting to know them as people, just as they must get to know him as a person.

EXPERIENCE OF THE SECULAR

It is in the small group of laymen that the preacher will find his research team. They are more in touch with the problems of the real world than he is. They know how difficult it is to relate the things they sing and say and hear on Sunday to life in the factory, the staff room, the shop, the office, the laboratory, on weekdays. The professional preacher has the Biblical and theological knowledge to bring to the discussion as resource material. But his knowledge remains, to some extent, disembodied until it can become incarnate in the daily experience of the lay Christians in the congregation. It is when this dialogue is really effective that the preacher begins to be able to proclaim an effective Gospel of the new life which Christ brings.

And this is where the lay preacher should have his big contribution to bring. The Free Churches have been pioneers in Britain in the use of laymen as preachers. Historically this has arisen from their conviction that the Holy Spirit calls whom He will to preach the Word of God, and that the Spirit cannot be controlled by any ordinances of men. In practice, notably in the Methodist Church, lay preachers have been called and trained because of the shortage of ordained men. It used to be said that five out of seven of the pulpits in Methodist Churches in England were occupied by laymen each Sunday.

More recently, the Church of England has made increasing use of Lay Readers, though the term 'lay' has been officially dropped. It is probable that this increasing emphasis on the ministry of the laity is brought about to a large extent because of the growing shortage of clergy available to keep the parishes adequately staffed. Changes seem to have happened for pragmatic reasons, rather than out of any deep conviction about the lay ministry. Yet it is becoming increasingly common for laity (and not only those who are accredited readers or local preachers) to speak from the pulpit from time to time.

THE LAY MINISTRY

Is there a special evangelistic ministry which the laity have to perform if given the opportunity? Too often, lay preachers have tended to become pale imitations of the clergy, even to the extent of using clerical voice and mannerisms. They are generally treated as stop-gap preachers who are allowed to mount the pulpit steps so long as there are not enough ministers to go round. Yet there must be aspects of the Gospel message which lay men and women are able to proclaim out of their experience which makes their contribution to the Church's evangelistic ministry different from and complementary to that of the ordained ministry.

At the moment, the kind of training given to lay readers and preachers is not very helpful. The syllabus tends to be a watered-down version of the subjects which candidates for ordination are expected to study. Is it really necessary for the lay preacher to have to know a great deal about third century heresies, the history of the Book of Common Prayer, or the ins and outs of ecclesiastical history?

He is being trained to serve the Church of today. He should be given basic knowledge on how to study the Bible: but a do-it-yourself kit of Bible Study method is more important than detailed knowledge about the authorship of Genesis or Habbakuk. He should be helped to understand what theology is all about, and particularly he should discover something of the exhilaration of the contemporary theological debate. He should be helped to understand the kind of way Christians approach ethical problems, with only enough history of ethics to help him to discuss the moral problems of today with some insight and intelligence. And he should be given some picture of the Church of today, on the assumption that the contemporary Church is likely to be of more interest for contemporaries than what has gone before. In particular, he should know something of the modern missionary situation, of the present state of unity discussion and negotiation, and of the movement towards renewal in every part of Christendom. All this should be firmly given within the context of the world-wide Church and not just of his own denomination. The training of laity (and for that matter of parsons) ought not to be done exclusively by clergy!

A consideration of the ministry of the laity ties up with the discussion now proceeding in a number of Churches about the role of the Diaconate. Even though it is right that serious thought should be given to the nature of the third order in our present situation, it would nevertheless be a tragedy if the preaching ministry were to be confined absolutely to those who in some way have received ordination. There are laymen who, by nature of their Christian commitment in the secular world, have a message of great relevance to bring to their fellows. They would claim that their Baptism into the Universal Church, and their experience of Christ in the world in which they live, provide them with all the credentials they need. Many find this kind of lay witness far more powerful than the utterances of professional preachers, whether clerical or lay.

CONTACTS WITH PEOPLE

The pulpit is not the only place where the Gospel can be proclaimed by word of mouth. Other opportunities for direct evangelism occur in the on-going ministry of the local Church. Even in these days when the Church as an institution is clearly losing much of her influence, there remain many occasions, notably at baptism, marriage and burial, when the clergy come into contact with people who are often only nominally linked with the Christian community. These are the very times when the Good News is most readily heard, if it can be seen to be relevant to the particular occasion. To write this is a platitude. Yet it is hard to believe that the evangelistic opportunities of these occasions are really being used to the full.

Here again it must be asked whether this is not another point where clergy and laity should be working together in the task of evangelism. A couple bringing their baby to baptism might be more interested in what another young married couple are trying to do about the religious upbringing of their children than in the professional exhortation of the vicar. Certainly lay people have a big part to play in preparation for marriage, as Churches have discovered when they have tried to take this part of their evangelistic ministry seriously by collaborating with the local marriage guidance council. Candidates for confirmation and Church membership continue to dwindle year by year. Even more alarming are the numbers who fall away after they have made some kind of commitment to the Church. This may well be because, on reflection, they discover that the Church is not worth being committed to. But it is certainly also due to the fact that few

Churches have given very much thought to the further education of their young people. This is discussed on a later page.

THE WRITTEN WORD

We also have to ask whether the fullest possible use has been made of the written word. Church magazines are still widely read, though their contents are generally sadly trivial. They are useful for providing information about mothers' meetings and jumble sales, but not much else. In some dioceses and areas, attempts have been made to present Christian news and views in a tabloid form. Coventry's *Shire and Spire*, Worcester's *Diocesan Messenger* (an uninspiring title) and Liverpool's *Catholic Pictorial* (the most tabloid of them all) are three examples amongst many. There is little evidence of their evangelistic influence. Here again their main interest seems to lie in the fact that they contain local information and gossip. A certain number of journals of general interest (notably women's magazines) contain regular articles by clergymen. Here is a chance to present the Gospel to a large readership, though the ministry exercised through these columns seems to be primarily one of comfort rather than of prophetic challenge.

Of greater interest is the growing number of paperback books on religion. The Churches in Britain owe a great debt to publishing houses for real pioneer work in evangelism by the written word. Works by some of the best modern expositors of the Christian Faith, such as C. S. Lewis, William Barclay, J. B. Phillips and Gerald Vann, have become easily and cheaply available. And a great impression has been created by rather more 'off-beat' books such as *The Cross and the Switchblade*[1] which the blurb on the cover describes as 'the thrilling true story of a country preacher's fight against teenage crime in

[1] David Wilkerson, Spire Books.

big city slums'. The rather naïve pietism of the author deeply involved in the world of the adolescent delinquent made a more profound impact on many readers than the more sophisticated rationality of most books of popular apologetics. Unfortunately, religious paper-backs do not seem to be generally on display in bookshops except those which specialize in 'religious literature', or those which are big enough to have a number of different departments. Nor can it be said that the Churches have done as much as they could to back up their allies in these publishing houses by displaying and recommending recent publications.

THE BROADCAST WORD

The preaching of the Gospel has always had a privileged place on radio and television. In fact, this policy of protected 'mainstream' religious broadcasting in Britain may have prevented the best use of this medium for evangelism. We tend either to get comfortable programmes of popular hymn singing, or discussions between the inevitable parson, psychiatrist and social worker, which are often ill-prepared, too short, and please nobody. Nothing appears to raise the wrath of the British public more quickly than the presentation of a viewpoint on radio and television which goes against established religious orthodoxy. That is what, for example, Professor G. W. H. Lampe discovered when he attempted to discuss with some seriousness the historical problem of the Resurrection narratives in an Easter Day programme.

The other reason for the disappointing results of religious broadcasting has been the comparatively low budgets within which the producers have had to work. It would be interesting to know the comparative costs of the annual sports output by B.B.C. and Independent Television, and the cost of their religious programmes. This is not to say that we ought to begrudge what is spent on sports programmes. It is to day-dream about what might be achieved if the same budgetary provision, technical skill and programme time could be made available to presenting the Gospel to the modern world. Yet we may, at least, be grateful that, in Britain, religious organizations have been unable to buy time on the air for evangelistic programmes. Experience in other countries where this is allowed does not suggest that Christian organizations can make any better use of the medium than commercial or artistic ones.

The development of local radio in England over the last few years offers some interesting opportunities, though it is too early to make any assessment of what has been achieved. It may be that the Churches, working in closest possible collaboration with the technical and production staffs of their local radio stations, will be able to make new discoveries of the possibilities in the use of radio. For all the talk of the withdrawal of the Church, there are still many listening ears if only we could know what to say and how to say it.

MISSIONS

We have been discussing the task of evangelism within the context of the total mission of the Church. Sermons, books and articles, radio and television, all have their place in the ministry of the Word. But what about 'missions' in the sense in which this word was once popularly used? It is already clear that Mission must not be confused with 'missions'. Yet is there still a place for missions in the evangelistic strategy of the Church either locally or in a wider area? Bishop Hensley Henson once wrote to a vicar, who asked about the advisability of holding a mission, that such things were 'superfluous in a well-worked parish, and mischievous in an ill-worked one.'[1] There is obvious truth here. The Gospel cannot be

[1] *Letters* of Herbert Hensley Henson, ed. E. F. Braley, S.P.C.K., 1950, p. 47.

proclaimed by an endless series of evangelistic stunts. But did Hensley Henson over-simplify? Most people would believe that whilst the total role of the Church in the worship of God and in its consequent service to man is to be evangelistic, yet there is a real place for the specific proclamation of the Gospel in campaigns especially focused for this purpose. Within the continuing mission of God, the Church needs from time to time to preach missions.

The purpose of such campaigns is not to revive dead Churches, although they sometimes seem to be used as desperate last minute attempts at spiritual artificial respiration when the corpse has obviously stopped breathing. It is doubtful whether these operations add significantly to membership numbers. After a temporary improvement, numbers fairly quickly return to their former situation. But such campaigns, carefully planned and organized, can help the Church itself to quicken the tempo of its life and work, and to turn its vision away from internal ecclesiastical preoccupations to the world for whose sake Christ has called it into being.

BILLY GRAHAM'S THRUST

What about the great campaigns promoted by the Billy Graham organization and by less ambitious evangelists such as Dr. Eric Hutchings and his team? It is difficult to come to a balanced judgment on such phenomena with their blending of old-fashioned evangelism and modern high pressure sales techniques. Their supporters make extravagant claims for their effectiveness. They quote the vast crowds which pour into Earl's Court and elsewhere night after night whilst a campaign is in progress. They issue figures of those who have 'decided for Christ' and 'come forward'. These figures are impressive until further questions are asked about how they are arrived at and what sort of people they include. How many people are counted more than once? How many of those who 'decide' are in fact already committed in one way or another to the Christian cause? The Billy Graham meetings seem to be largely supported by bus-loads of the faithful drawn from all over the country by a brilliantly contrived cult of personality ('Hear Billy Graham') and by highly efficient organization. The majority would appear to come as 'fans' rather than as seekers.

More seriously, how much does this Bible-centred ballyhoo, with its immense emotional pressure on personal decision, really reflect the Gospel of the Word made flesh? And how much does it create in some minds a misleadingly false impression of what the Christian Faith is all about? Even those who in the past have been loudest in their support for these great campaigns are now beginning to ask questions about their real effectiveness. Perhaps they are an outworn method, to be discarded now with gratitude for service rendered in the past. And gratitude there must be, for only a churlish partisanship could deny that people like Billy Graham have been used by God, or that there are not many who can speak with deep conviction and reality about their experience of conversion following one of these campaigns.

Even if such evangelistic missions have had their day, we must not allow this to blind us to the fact that in some form or another there may still be a need for 'Missions' in the local church. Certainly there is need for inspiration, for a sense of urgency, and for a renewal of trust in the Living God who is ready to use us for His purpose in the place where we live. We need to evaluate with care and honesty all that is known to be good in traditional evangelistic campaigns, and to see what new application they can be given today so that the Church may not flinch from the task entrusted to it.

An eloquent advocate of the traditional mission in slightly modern dress is Dr. Cuthbert Bardsley, Bishop of Coventry. In the autumn of 1968, as part of the Jubilee

Celebrations in his Diocese, he issued a Call to Mission. For ten days Coventry Cathedral was packed to the doors, with four over-flow meetings in neighbouring halls. The Bishop, with his customary enthusiasm, sought to justify this exercise both in broadcasts and in the columns of *The Times*. His apologia for the mission today is worth taking seriously.

The Bishop 'respects those who deeply believe that in the modern situation the direct confrontation of people with the claims of the Gospel is no longer in accord with the thought patterns of our age, which prefers dialogue to proclamation'. He fully understands those who 'find in the sight of humble personal service and involvement in social concern more effective Christian witness than the sound of the voice which proclaims "Thus saith the Lord".' But the Bishop goes on to champion the value of the spoken word for today. 'There must come a time when the believer must be prepared to say what he believes and why, to take his stand upon it, and to offer the good news of the Gospel to the world of his day.' After a careful examination of his Jubilee Mission, the Bishop concludes: 'First, the day of mission in its various forms is not over. Indeed, a new one may be dawning. I believe that many of those who have been involved in that dialogue and questioning of Christian Fundamentals which has been a feature – a necessary one – of the religious life of the island for the past decade, are in many instances themselves coming to see that there is yet a place for those who will say "Thus saith the Lord".'

CONVERSION

What is the end product of evangelism? Many would say that it is to convert men and women to Christ. But what is the meaning of conversion? Conversion is part of the process by which a man becomes a Christian. A Christian is a man who sees the purpose of God in the life and work of Christ, and who then accepts Christ's way for himself.

Men make this act of acceptance in many different ways. Professor J. G. Davies has written 'The attempt to dragoon souls into conformity with a single and, in fact, none too healthy pattern of spiritual experience, disregards the divine means by which the spirit of God actually works'. This is an important warning. Conversion has tended to become a vested interest of a particular section of the Christian world. It is a naïve assumption that a particular psychological process is the only valid entrance into Christian experience. At worst, it can become an appalling piece of religious one-upmanship, with the self-satisfied assumption that only those who can quote time, place and occasion for 'conversion' are truly Christian, and that everyone else (however devout) has not yet caught the real thing. With adolescents this point of view is particularly damaging. Having entered the new Jerusalem with the sound of many trumpets, they wake to discover that the streets of the heavenly city are paved with precisely the same material as the place they thought they had left behind. They had been promised an escape both from themselves and from the world, only to discover a growing suspicion that they were still very much themselves, and living in the same familiar places.

Somebody once said that conversion is a double event. A man must be converted from self-centredness and world-centredness to a way of life which puts Christ firmly in the middle. But as soon as this is done, he must be converted back into the world. For this new-found experience of fellowship with Christ does not become valid until it has begun to work itself out in all the relationships of everyday life in the world. Far from being an invitation to other-worldliness, conversion is the process by which a man sees that every part of life must be brought within the orbit of God's reconciling love, as seen and made available in Christ. Conversion is not to be an escape from sex, politics, social concern, art, or the enjoyment of life. It is to see and to experience every part of life with a new clarity. Nor is this the superficial optimism of those who go through life with bright 'I'm saved' smiles on their faces, but rather those who see in every aspect of the human situation the agony and the ecstasy which is Good Friday and Easter Day.

The challenge of the word 'conversion' cannot be ignored. In our anxiety to avoid the more embarrassing and inadequate manifestations of 'twice-born Christianity', we must avoid going to the other extreme and ignoring entirely the place of decision in the evangelistic work of the church.

Throughout the New Testament there is always a sense of urgency to turn away from the self-centredness of sin and darkness, and to receive the freedom and light which Christ has come to bring. We need not subscribe to any particular theory of conversion to see the power of this Gospel. But we must be certain that this Gospel is never restricted to the limits of a personal insurance policy, or narrowed to 'soul saving'. We are entrusted with the message of reconciling the whole man in the whole of his life with God. The disciples of the Man for others must see in conversion a new commitment in themselves for others. This is the mission of the Church, and it must be seen to be so. But power can only come as each member begins to discover in himself what this reconciliation with God is all about.

6

OUTLOOK ON YOUTH

EVERYTHING DEPENDS ON THE next generation. Will
they reject the Church or will they reform it? We cannot
precisely foresee the future: nor can we determine it.
Either the reformation of the Church as we know it, or
its extermination, might be in the plan and purpose of
God. All we can do is to present as faithfully as we can our
understanding of the Gospel to the next generation, and
invite them to share in the Church, not as it now is, but
as it might become. In this and the following chapter
we discuss four separate, though related, aspects of the
Church to the next generation. In the first section there is
an attempt to examine 'youth strategy' in the local
parish or congregation. The second deals with the
relationship between the Church and the youth service,
both statutory and voluntary. This is based on the particular system as it has evolved in England, though doubtless
it has some relevance elsewhere. The next section (in
chapter 7) looks at the problem of handing down moral
attitudes from one generation to another, and examines
particularly the traditional Christian ethic regarding
sexual intercourse before marriage. The final section
discusses the involvement of the Church of England in the
state educational system, and questions whether this is a
responsible way of fulfilling the Christian mission to young
people.

I

TEENAGE DOUBTS

Whatever may be the background of their religious
upbringing, most intelligent and sensible young people
go through a period of questioning and doubt sometime
in their mid-teens. This is the process by which they move
from a second-hand faith (that of their parents, clergy, or
Sunday School teachers) to a religion of their own. It is
the period when religious truths, which until now they
have seen only as Bible texts or statements of dogma, have
to be matched up against the real problems of life which
they are beginning to face.

Of course, there are some teenagers who do not go
through this period of uneasiness. It may be that they
have been subjected to such high-pressure dogmatism
that they have come to believe that it is wrong to question
the religious noises made by their clergy and elders. Or
they have such a conventional and superficial concept of
religion that it remains untouched by the real questions
of life. But for most young people there must be a time of
genuine reappraisal. With many, it happens not long
after Confirmation. With some, it seems to follow the
O-level year. With all, it is to be welcomed by adults,
and dealt with sympathetically and intelligently. For,
although the Tennyson dictum about there being more
faith in honest doubt than in half the creeds has been
over-quoted (and sometimes misquoted), it certainly has
a measure of truth as far as the adolescent is concerned.
There is more hope for the 17-year-old who is restless,
doubtful and questioning, than for the goody-goody
conformist who sticks to all the ecclesiastical rules but
who has not begun to search for a living and relevant
religion.

It is an essential part of growing up today that young

F

people should go through a process in which the accepted dogmas of Church and society are radically questioned. Can we go on believing what older people tell us we ought to believe? Can we go on behaving in the way that older people tell us we ought to behave? These are vital questions. It is not for adults to prevent young people from asking such questions as searchingly as they can. It is certainly our job to give them the equipment by which they can find their own answers. But it is not for us to discourage the questioning. If we try to do this, we may promote a dead kind of orthodoxy in the next generation, but we shall not encourage a living faith.

Not long ago I was responsible for two B.B.C. schools broadcasts on the subject of the Crucifixion and Resurrection of Christ. I recorded two spontaneous discussions with boys and girls of 16 and 17 in schools in Lancashire and Essex. In these broadcasts, listeners heard serious and intelligent youngsters questioning the necessity of the Crucifixion ('Why did Jesus have to die?') and casting doubts on the historical facts of the Resurrection ('It didn't actually happen like the Bible said, but it's an inspiring story, nevertheless'). A number of adults, including clergy, wrote letters of shocked protest to the B.B.C. and to myself. How dare we let young people say such things, or question the official dogmas of the Church? They should have been contradicted flatly, and certainly not allowed to air their views over the radio. What the critics failed to realize was that not only were those young people being honest and sincere in their comments, but they were reflecting the theological debate going on inside and outside the Church today, but which is rarely reflected in sermons or Sunday School lessons.

We must expect a Church, which is alive to the real world in which it is set, to be in a state of ferment. For the Christian faith is based on the belief that in history God entered right into our human situation. And during the thirty years of His life in Palestine, Jesus was a man of

His times, using the same language as other men, and
sharing their ideas about the world of men and affairs.
In every generation the Church is called to be part of the
the real world, interpreting the eternal truths committed
to it in the language and thought of each succeeding
generation. Christians are therefore called to take change
seriously. For change calls them to re-examine their faith
in the light of their own situation. In times of rapid
change, such as ours, that re-examination is bound to be
radical and painful. It is only a dead Church, with a
nervous system decayed by age, which is insensitive to the
changes going on all round it. It is therefore not surprising
that boys and girls who have grown up in this exciting
and bewildering post-war world are bound to ask whether
the things which Christians believe and do have any
meaning for their world. When they go into a church or
Bible class, they may well feel that they are stepping back
into some unreal world of the past, where the questions
of today are politely but firmly ignored.

Modern science and technology have revolutionized
our view of the world, and our ability to control it. The
Bible, as boys and girls meet it in religious lessons in day
schools, and in church and Bible class on Sunday, seems
to belong to a different age. Before science provided the
reasons, there was room for superstition. Before technology
gave the know-how, there had to be a reliance on magic.
Is there not evidence of both magic and superstition in the
Bible passages which are solemnly read from the brass
eagle in church Sunday by Sunday? Boys and girls want
to know how all this ties up with O-level physics or A-level
biology. One Ascension Day I had the job of preaching
to a boys' school. I tried to impress upon them that the
Christian faith does not demand that once upon a time a
man literally floated up into the air and disappeared.
I pointed out that the concept of 'up' has to do with
authority and kingship. When they say that the headmaster is 'over' the school, they do not mean that he is

sitting on the roof! So Ascension Day speaks of the kingship of Christ over the whole world. But immediately after the sermon, the hymn was announced and the boys rose to sing lustily:

> Hail the day that sees him rise
> To His throne above the skies.

and I wondered, as we sang it, what these young people could have made of this strange Christian faith of ours.

TEENAGE REVOLT

Much of the religious teenage revolt arises from this apparent double-think of the Church, which tries to present a living Gospel to the modern world in the language and idiom of the past age. But there are other, less intellectual, factors which contribute to the revolt, and they are even more significant. One is undoubtedly the amateurishness and slipshod character of public worship. Too many services are inadequately prepared. The music is often unattractive and uninspiring. Lessons are often unintelligible, either because the passages are obscure or because the reading is inaudible or mannered. Most young people say that they enjoy the sermon better than any other part of the service, but they – like their elders – are not infrequently disappointed with the fare that they are given. All this contrasts sadly with television, where the most trivial serial or pop programme is produced with a care and professionalism which makes so much public worship seem dowdy. And where public worship is inadequate, the congregation itself is unable to communicate a sense of enthusiasm or purpose to the younger members. Worship appears to be a matter of dull habit.

A deeper factor still is the question of authority. The Christian faith has usually been presented to the young on some kind of authoritarian basis. They must believe this dogma or that morality because 'the Bible says so', or because 'the Church teaches it'. But not only is the authority of the Bible and Church open to considerable question today; the whole basis of authority is being challenged in the modern world. Young people, who in their middle teens must be expected to rebel against authority as a matter of course, will quickly raise questions about the validity of the religious truths which are being communicated to them.

CONCERN FOR THE WORLD

Revolt is not the only characteristic of the modern teenager. Along with the rejection of much that the adult world stands for, there is growing concern that the world should become a better and a fairer place. Behind much of the student rebellion that is sweeping the universities and colleges of the world, there is more than an adolescent desire to be against the government. Dramatic changes are being initiated on the insistence of the young. Recently the vice-chancellors and student representatives of British universities put their signatures to a joint statement which meets students' demands for participation and representation on university governing bodies and for reforms in disciplinary procedures and methods of examination. This represents a revolution in the history of education, and it is only the beginning of an important new chapter. For if the demand for participation is rightly met at the university level, how long will it be before similar demands are made at the top level of the secondary school? And what will this mean for the Church in its education of the adolescent? There is already a union for sixth-formers in process of formation.

Some will see in all this further evidence that young people are growing too big for their boots. Certainly it does not always do them good to be flattered and exploited, as they sometimes are, both by commercial interests and by 'with it' clerics. But this must not blind us to the fact that much of this earnest desire for participation springs from a genuine concern for the well-being of the community. The long continuation of the war in Vietnam and colour discrimination in Rhodesia and South Africa arouses more passion in the growing generation today than the rise of Hitler or the toleration of massive unemployment did in their parents.

There is plenty of other evidence to show that young people today are learning to care about the world in which they are growing up. In the comparatively short time since the inauguration of the Shelter campaign for the homeless, a great part of the massive sum raised has been on the initiative of young people. In fact, Shelter has almost become a youth organization with the one object of expressing practical concern for the slum dwellers of our land. Christian Aid and Oxfam have also attracted young people. Folk-song competitions, sponsored marches, hunger meals and much else have been used, not only to raise money for these good causes, but to draw public attention to them.

INTEREST IN PEOPLE

Nor is all this just a question of extracting money from the pockets of other people. In youth organizations and schools there is an increasing response to personal service. There is a great story to be written of the experience of boys and girls who set out to 'do good' to the house-bound old folk or the handicapped in wheel chairs, and who found this developed quickly into a richly rewarding fellowship.

The point is that most young people growing up are fascinated by personal relationships of all kinds. A surprising number, when asked to say the priorities which influence their choice of work, will put 'working with people' far in advance of wages or security. More and more of them want to travel, hitch-hiking or camping in foreign countries, in order to meet new people face to face. And much of their discussion about sex morality springs from a suspicion that their elders are frightened of sex and unwilling to take personal relationships seriously.

All this is of immense importance as we come to consider the mission of the Church amongst teenagers today. For the interest they have in people and personal relationships is one which they share with the Bible. The Bible sees throughout an inextricable link between man's relationship with his fellow-men and his relationship with God. When Jesus inaugurated His ministry with a campaign of practical compassion, people marvelled how much He understood 'what was in man'. Later He was to teach His disciples that acts of mercy done for the sick, the hungry, the destitute and the prisoner, were acts of mercy done for Him. And, later still, one of His closest disciples was to insist that anyone who claims to love God while hating his brother is a liar.

YOUTH STRATEGY

It is clear that the ways in which boys and girls can be helped to care for other people is of basic importance as we consider how to bring the message of the Gospel to the younger generation today. This must be our starting point. And a number of practical considerations arise from it.

First, we must recognize and thank God for the spirit of Christ seen in so much teenage humanism. If we want 'hymns' about the modern world and its needs, we are more likely to find them in the repertoire of Pete Seeger, Bob Dylan, or Julie Felix, than in our traditional hymnbooks. Too many hymns, with their emphasis on personal salvation, are essentially self-centred. Many modern folksongs breathe a more Christian spirit. Those who have the responsibility of religious education amongst adolescents must make it their business to discover as much as they can of what young people are singing, thinking, and

doing. It often may not seem to have much to do with
conventional religion, but when looked at with eyes
trained to see things as the Bible sees them, there may be
much to thank God for. Too often the Church seems only
interested in people who do things in 'churchy' ways. Our
first evangelistic task with young people is to show our
interest in the things which interest them.

WHAT'S GOING ON?

Secondly, we must recognize that we are not likely to get
young people interested in God until we have first got
them interested in other people. A real knowledge of what
is happening all around us is a basic prerequisite of
evangelism. It is important to ask what part all this
plays in the programmes of Christian youth clubs, or in
the syllabus of Bible class or Sunday School. However
desirable it may be to learn about the saints and heroes of
the past, it is even more important that young people
should come to see that, most of all, Christians are concerned about what is going on in the world here and now.
Too often we give the impression of only being interested
in the days gone by. Many of the 'yarns for boys and
girls' which still provide the basis for Bible class work
have little relevance for the present day. The youth and
education departments of the major missionary societies,
as well as Christian Aid and other organizations, can
provide plenty of first-class material in this field. This was
well recognized by the bishops at the 1968 Lambeth
Conference, who expressed their gratitude for 'the
intensified interest of young people in human welfare',[1]
were conscious of 'the value of their informed insights',
and, recognizing the need to involve them in decision-
making in both secular and ecclesiastical society, 'reques-
ted provinces, dioceses, and parishes to promote this
involvement in every possible way'.

[1] Lambeth Conference 1968, Report and Resolutions, S.P.C.K., p. 38.

Thirdly, as we discuss openly and frankly the wide range of personal relationship questions which interest them, we must be prepared to help young people to see the Biblical and theological truths upon which answers to moral problems must be built. This means that the teachers and youth leaders who deal with adolescents must be prepared to devote time to hard and honest study themselves. You can no longer hand out to teen-agers neat pre-packaged answers. We are called to dig deeper.

Finally, practical experience of service should be made available to young people as a necessary preparation for receiving the Gospel. When they have learnt to love their fellow-men through service, there is a greater chance that their hearts will be opened to receive the personal ex-perience of the love of God. Certainly it is better that boys and girls should be out and about amongst their fellow-men than hanging about the church and the sacristy. Over-preoccupation with ecclesiastical things in a teenager is a danger sign. Social service projects should therefore have a real part in youth work, in the senior Sunday School and Bible class syllabus, and in preparation for Confirmation. If it is objected that this is mere human-ism, it must be pointed out that in Jesus Christ Himself we see the meaning of true humanism.

But what of the Church and young people? The Church is its own worst enemy. It speaks of itself in such splendid phrases as 'The Body of Christ' and 'The Divine Society'. In practice, it often appears drab, divided and unadventurous. More and more it seems, young people are fascinated by the claims of Christ, and are ready to take them seriously. Less and less are they ready to get in-volved in the Church. Of course young teenagers are well represented as churchgoers. They are gregarious by nature and the church provides them with a good meeting-place. But once they begin to become adult, church loyalty wanes. Advanced studies, new work, courtship and home-making, are the new centres of interest; and what goes on in church seems to have little relevance to them. It becomes apparent that Sunday School, Confirmation classes, and church-going have given them little equipment for life in the real world. So it is that many of our more intelligent young people are attracted to the present 'non-church' movement, and are seriously questioning whether church membership should be considered a necessary part of Christian discipline.

Those who believe that Christianity without the Church is a false trail have the New Testament on their side; but if young people are to be genuinely involved in the life of the Church a good deal of fresh thinking is needed.

GENERATION GAPS

Everything must be done to break down the barrier between old and young, and to enable young people to share in decision-making in the parish. This is not easy, partly because the young are often immature in judgment, partly because older people tend to cling on to all the key jobs. Furthermore, when younger people have achieved membership of the parochial church council or church meeting, they tend to be patronized by their elders rather than treated as equal partners. Yet the Church, which has reconciliation as its central theme, ought to be the place where the generation gap is successfully bridged.

It is, however, not so much in the formal structures of church government as in the various informal groupings in the parish where young and old can meet most effectively. Of course, there remains a place for specific youth work in the parish, but it becomes increasingly essential that Bible study and discussion groups, lay training and Retreat week-ends and such like, should be real cross-sections of the whole parish, with the young taking their full share of the responsibility. It must be genuine responsibility, and not just the 'playing at being churchwardens' in the Junior Church!

PRAYER

Further, the Church must show young people that it sides with them in their concern for humanity. In many churches prayers are singularly unimaginative, and give little impression that the Church exists to serve the world. Even today prayers are often limited to intercessions for the Queen, for clergy and people, and for vaguely defined virtues. No wonder that to many young people it all seems just a way of propping up the Establishment and giving pious respectability to the *status quo*. The success among young people of such books as Michel Quoist's *Prayers of Life*[1] suggests there is a hunger for the kind of intercession which makes sense. Prayer which really invites the worshipper to share in our Lord's agony for His world will probably have a greater impact on the young than any number of sermons. They make it clear that the Church is called to be the servant of the world, and not an escape from it into a pious cloud cuckoo land.

Prayer must lead to service. There is plenty of evidence to show that boys and girls find the way to a living faith through personal service. They will have no faith in a Church which does not bear the marks of the Suffering Servant. They will rightly conclude that an inward-looking Church is just not worth belonging to. This is why practical service for such organizations as Christian Aid and Shelter should find an increasing place in the syllabus of senior Sunday Schools, Confirmation preparation classes, and church youth organizations. After all, it is really more important to learn to serve in the name of Christ than it is to know how many Sundays there are in Advent, or the colours of the altar frontals at the various seasons of the year.

PROBLEMS AND PROJECTS

But service will raise all the big questions, for no one

[1] Gill, Dublin.

can work with the physically or mentally handicapped without coming face to face with the deepest questions about life and death. No one can see the world through the eyes of Shelter or Christian Aid without coming up against the problem of evil in the world, and the involvement of the Church with it. In face of the world's real problems, little talks on the Apostle's Creed, or 'what the Church teaches' are frankly not much use. There has to be honest enquiry, a willingness to wrestle with the real problems, and an approach to truth in which hope is mixed with humility. However good the lessons were in Sunday School or Confirmation class, by the time boys and girls reach the age of 16 these are likely to seem irrelevant, or to have been forgotten altogether.

By and large the Church has not faced up to the problems of the further education of its young people. For many in the Church of England, Confirmation is still the passing-out parade. But such further education needs to be approached with imagination. Out-of-date classroom methods only spell boredom. The experience of the Christian Education Movement, and the insights of modern group method need to be examined seriously in our work with adolescents. Residential week-ends or informal get-togethers in one another's homes are likely to be more effective than the Bible class held every Tuesday evening in an ugly and draughty vestry.

There are many methods to be explored. But what is certain is that we are failing to help many of our boys and girls towards a relevant faith when on the threshold of adult life they are most in need of it.

Basic to the life of the Church and its evangelistic task is the experience of worship. Here is our most difficult and most rewarding task in our work with young people. How do we set about it? Already there has been a good deal of experimental youth worship. It has become a common experience to plug electric guitars into the sanctuary, and to blast the ears of the congregation with a familiar hymn belted out in beat tempo. All experiments are useful, but it must be admitted that much of this so-called twentieth century church music is more reminiscent of Ivor Novello than the Beatles, with words which are often astonishingly trite and banal.

The modern folk-song movement is more hopeful. And collections such as *Faith, Folk and Clarity*[1] include material which helps young people to sing with relevance about the real problems of the world which must be the concern of the Christian. In particular, Sydney Carter has made a great contribution here, and the kind of songs he writes should have a place in every senior Sunday School and Church youth programme.

But there also needs to be the encouragement of much more experiment in worship amongst young people. This is best done by the group project method in which worship is evolved out of much thought and discussion. Here dance and drama will take their place among the more traditional elements of worship, and modern Pop and Folk Music will appear to be as normal as *Hymns Ancient and Modern*! For there is no doubt that much of our worship is imprisoned in an old-fashioned middle-class culture, and it is a culture which makes little appeal to the younger generation.

In its work with young people today, the Church is facing a time of tremendous and exciting opportunity. But it will miss this opportunity if it is not prepared to combine a loyalty to the Faith with an ability to think fearlessly and to act adventurously.

II

THE CHURCH AND THE YOUTH SERVICE

In spite of all the talk about the declining influence of religion, the Christian Churches remain a major partner

[1] ed. Peter Smith, Galliard Publications.

in the modern Youth Service in Britain. Of the 26 constituent member organizations of the Standing Conference of National Voluntary Youth Organizations, over half are of religious foundation and work on a specifically Christian or Jewish basis. Of the other organizations such as Scouts, Guides, the National Association of Boys' Clubs, and the National Association of Youth Clubs, there is within their affiliation a high proportion of Church Clubs. In addition to this, there is an immense number of Youth Clubs attached to churches of all denominations which have no national affiliation. Many do not even appear in the local youth organizations handbook. No one knows how many such groups there are in existence.

But the Churches have never been concerned solely with providing a service for their own young members. There is a long tradition in all denominations of open club work. Perhaps there has been a certain element of missionary propaganda here. Give young people table-tennis, billiards, a record-player, or a gymnasium, and hope to be able to inject a religious message in the process. It is natural that those who believe that they have found a way of life which makes sense should want to pass this on. To many people, their faith in God is the biggest thing they have to give to boys and girls growing up. To provide recreation, amusement, or even instruction, whilst ignoring the basic issues of faith and conduct is to do a great disservice to the young people with whom we are concerned.

Yet amongst young people and many adults there is a healthy suspicion of 'do-gooders' or of organizations which have strings attached. The Churches themselves have often felt that they need find no further justification for an open Youth Club than that it meets a real human need. It is not long since the Churches spent much time and money in distributing coal and groceries to the poor and needy. This was not bribery to get people to come to church; it was caring for people in need for their own sakes. Few boys and girls today lack the material things necessary for reasonable living, but many suffer from an inner loneliness and frustration which a good Youth Club can help to alleviate. The Good Samaritan did not seek any return for his act of charity other than the knowledge that he was helping a man in his moment of need. This remains the only justification for the Church's entry into open youth work. Of course, the local church is wise to concentrate on its own members if the wider constituency is being catered for by voluntary organizations or the statutory services. Furthermore, it is dangerous to embark on open youth work without adequate premises and skilled leadership. But where there is a need and where leadership and equipment are available, the Churches still have a job to do in this field. This is part and parcel of their mission.

UNATTACHED YOUTH

But in recent years there has been a new development in youth service. This is work with the so-called 'unattached' young people, and it has developed interesting parallels with some of the concepts of 'mission through involvement' described earlier in this book. At the conclusion of the standard text book on this subject, the authors write:

> We found the opportunity offered by the Honest to God debate of participating in the re-evaluation of the traditional values and standards, an important, indeed primary aid in making the necessary changes in our own attitudes and approaches. We felt that without this background much of what we believe we were able to offer young people would have been impossible.[1]

PATRONIZING OUT

It is worth examining in more detail this new approach to youth work, and to discover what it has in common with

[1] George W. Goetschius and M. Joan Tash, *Working with Unattached Youth*, Routledge and Kegan Paul, p. 328.

the contemporary theological discussion. For a long time, youth workers have admitted that their efforts only touch, at most, about a third of the adolescent population in England. What about the other two-thirds? Many of these have no need to avail themselves of the opportunities the youth service offers to them. They are continuing their education until the late teens or early twenties, their jobs offer them adequate satisfaction and recompense, and they are able to move into adult life making satisfactory relationships both with their peers and with the community at large. But there are others who are unable to achieve such satisfactory relationships. They are either unable, or unwilling, to accept the help of youth organizations or other social or educational agencies. Some of them develop strong anti-social tendencies and may drift into delinquency. At best, they are failing to make the most of themselves as human beings, and of the positive things which society can offer them. How can such young people be helped without being patronized or dragooned by the older generation? This is the problem which the unattached workers set themselves. It is, in the wide sense of the word, a problem about evangelism – the bringing of the good news of what life is all about to those who are in need of that news.

Working with Unattached Youth is the account of a project undertaken by the Y.W.C.A. in an inner-London borough. The focal point of the work was initially a mobile coffee stall where, during the first year, contact was established with about a hundred 'regulars'. The next two years of the project were occupied in developing these contacts in a number of sub-groups. At the same time, increasing opportunities for pastoral counselling opened up. A final year was needed for analysis, evaluation and the preparation of the report. Again and again in the pages of this book we are reminded of the on-going discussion on evangelism in the Church today. One primary emphasis is on the necessity of taking young people seriously for their own sakes, and the refusal to impose an alien cultural pattern upon them. In such passages as these we see the meaning of incarnation:

> The field workers not only followed the pattern created by the young people, but they learned to use it in order to be more effective in their service. Firstly they became part of the pattern in order to observe the young people, on the stall, in a café, coffee bar, or on a street corner. Secondly they used the casual meetings in the streets or in public houses to hear how Tom was getting on with his work or to listen to the grape-vine news.[1]

Is this not a reflection in contemporary terms of the method that Jesus Himself used? He became 'part of the pattern', even at the risk of being criticized as 'a glutton and a drunkard, a friend of tax collectors and sinners'.

Just as the Church has come to recognize that the world must provide the agenda, so these workers saw that the means of contact with the young people must be provided by the boys and girls themselves.

> Meeting people, talking, discussing, arguing, going out to the cinema or up the road together were just as much 'activities' as were table tennis tournaments or highly organized sports. ... Once we relaxed and accepted the material presented by the young people as activities, the talking, larking about, occasional trip and spontaneous interest, a full-scale programme developed, wider in scope than anything we had anticipated.[2]

And again, reminding us of the long apprenticeship of Jesus in His hidden years, the workers reported

> it took us a long time to come to terms with the natural patterns of mobility that were woven into the life of the young people.

Only with this kind of mobility and flexibility could the right kind of relationship between adults and young

---

[1] *op. cit.*, p. 61.
[2] *op. cit.*, pp. 63–4.

G

people be established. The Report strongly criticizes conventional youth work because it often seems more interested in preserving its own image and maintaining its own life as an institution than in meeting the needs of young people where they are and how they are. In many organizations certain degrees of conformity are demanded before young people can be accepted.

> The vested interests of the youth service agencies in established traditional programmes of service, moral allegiances and institutional structure make it difficult for them to alter their pattern of service without at the same time changing the nature of their service, the conditions on which it is offered, and their administrative structure.[1]

Might this not be applied with equal justice to the Church in the face of the challenge of greater mobility and flexibility if it is to be a worthwhile instrument of evangelism in the modern world?

> Clubs tend to demand a particular cultural conformity (usually middle-class) in exchange for the services given. In youth work their preoccupations about programme content, time, place and conditions, frequently based on a reasoning that youth work is about character training which includes being made to meet the conditions of service. Subscriptions, organized activities, rules and regulations, and ideas about loyalty are either not understood or are resented.[2]

It is difficult not to see a close parallel here between the rules of life urged upon young people at the time of Confirmation or reception into Church membership, or the 'obligations of churchmanship' sometimes issued by ecclesiastical authorities. The Christian life is often summed up in terms of 'subscriptions, organized activities, rules and regulations and ideas about loyalty'.

[1] *op. cit.*, p. 324.
[2] *op. cit.*, p. 127.

This study of youth work is deeply concerned with the establishment of right relationships across the generation and culture gaps. Here again, it provides variations on the Christian theme of reconciliation. Work with individuals and small groups is commended for the same reason which may make people in the Churches wish to move away from mass evangelism techniques to an approach on a more deeply personal level.

> The most urgent need was to make it possible for the individual field workers to choose two or three smaller groups from the larger network, and to try to work with them, providing more intensive service and creating within the group an atmosphere in which it might be possible for the young people to help each other.[1]

From this method of working, it was possible to begin to create the kind of relationship between the adult workers and the young, in which effective counselling could be given. And from this, came the creation of small groups in which the young people themselves could begin to help and support one another.

So we find in the comparatively restricted area of youth work precisely the same discoveries about 'mission' as are beginning to be made in the Churches. And these discoveries have a profoundly theological basis, capable of being expressed in totally non-theological language.

George Goetschius and Joan Tash only speak specifically about this at the very end of their book. It is on the final page that they conclude:

> As regards the Christian commitment in work of this type, we must point out that the changes we have described in the content of traditional concepts has not left the Church itself unaffected. The content of the 'Honest to God' debate is surely one indication of the change in emphasis in what Christians mean by 'authority' and 'discipline'. This is

[1] *op. cit.*, p. 45.

especially true of the concept of 'relationship' which is now seen as fundamental to the nature and content of Christian witness. The move with Bonhoeffer, Bultmann, and Tillich away from purely traditional forms, and implications of this for institutional change, is surely evidence of the Church's recognition of some of the kinds of changes we have been discussing. We must also remember that much of the youth work in the past was based on traditional concepts of character training with heavy moralistic overtones, which are even now in process of change within the Christian Church itself.

7

OUTLOOK ON EDUCATION

I

NOT LONG AGO THE national press carried reports of a speech by the Director of the Department of Venereology in the Middlesex Hospital, London. He was quoted as saying that there was more venereal disease in Britain today than in any peacetime period since the Restoration. The wave which then started lasted for about fifty years, and it was the middle-class which led the trend back to tighter sexual standards. Now, says the Director, the middle-class forms a significant proportion of new patients. Having said that with the present acute shortage of doctors there could be no hope of containing the disease if the present trend continues, he concluded:

> The best that can be done is to try to keep the disease at present level, and this in turn depends on a change in the moral climate which would reduce promiscuity.

MORAL MALAISE

But how possible is this change and how can it be brought about? In the sphere of moral malaise, no less than in medicine, an accurate diagnosis must be made before a remedy can be prescribed. But who can with certainty diagnose our present situation? Churchmen are quick to say that the root lies in the decline of religion. A religious faith, they claim, is no longer generally learned in infancy at home. Religious instruction in school often fails to get to the heart of the matter. The Churches no longer command the allegiance of the majority of young people. Sunday Schools are a declining influence. The Ten

Commandments are no longer considered a basic element in upbringing. Little wonder we have a moral decline. So clergy and church-minded laity often argue, and the argument can be made to sound convincing. Yet does this really take us to the heart of the matter?

On the other hand, books appear from time to time, written by 'sex-experts' who have little sympathy with the Church. Such writers enjoy making fun at the expense of St. Paul and St. Augustine. They blame the Christian Church for equating sex with sin, and for adding to the total unhappiness of mankind by confusing erotic pleasure with guilt. The Papal Encyclical, *Humanae Vitae*, has added grist to the mill. Little wonder, they say with evident approval, that men and women are powerfully attracted to the delightful pursuits which their priests and pastors tell them are wicked. This, too, can be made to sound convincing. But are the professional sceptics, any more than the traditional churchmen, helping us to get our morality straight?

Comparative morality is a dangerous and useless game. How sure can we be that one generation is better or worse than that which preceded it? Certainly every decade produces those who ask what young people are coming to nowadays. Yet it is hard to believe that there has been a continuous and steady decline since Adam! Today we have a growing number of sociologists eager to gain their degrees by putting the younger generation under a critical microscope. The youth of previous centuries were fortunate not to be subjected to the same close scrutiny, except from time to time by a Congreve, a Sterne, or a Hogarth. Even hard statistics now available of the incidence of illegitimacy, of V.D., must not be allowed to stampede us into sweeping generalization about 'young people today'.

Yet there are factors in the present situation which must be taken seriously and given careful examination. It is a commonplace to say that young people today grow up more quickly and more freely than ever before. A high standard of living, a decline in parental discipline, and greater mobility, all contribute to the present pattern of behaviour. As parked cars at night in the countryside around our big cities testify, the invention of the internal combustion engine did something for our morals as well as for our transport. The open (and sometimes blatant) sale of contraceptives in barbers' shops, 'surgical stores', or by post from so-called 'laboratories', may encourage a young man like the hero in *A Kind of Loving*[1] to persuade his girl to 'go all the way' because he feels himself to be adequately protected. Few novels today seem to be complete without a detailed running commentary on an act (or succession of acts) of fornication.

We are not likely to find an answer to the problem of changing the moral climate simply by repeating these familiar facts. For the very things which appear to aggravate the situation are also important positive factors in our society. Do we really want to give our young people less freedom? Do we not agree that basically the decline of parental discipline can be a gain and not a loss if it is used to create a more flexible relationship between the generations? Are not most of us seeking to relax censorship rather than to increase it? And can anyone seriously wish that contraceptives should be banned from public sale, despite the abuse to which they are put?

SEEKING AN ANSWER

It is no good simply wishing that we could put the clock back. We have to seek a working morality within the present social climate. And we have to admit that any honest examination of the arguments we have been in the habit of using in the past in order to convey morality (and especially Christian morality) look rather thin in the light of present-day thinking and experience.

[1] Sam Barstow, Penguin Books.

Little books on 'What Every Young Man (or Woman) Should Know' used to contain pious exhortations about purity, and quoted the appropriate text of Scripture on the evil consequences which would befall the sinner both in this world and the next. More practical (and more telling to the teenager than threats of a long-distance Hell) were hints, held out to a lesser or greater degree, of the risks of disease and unwanted children. There was even sometimes a suggestion that V.D. and illegitimacy were instruments which a just God used to punish the wrongdoer. Can we not detect in the present approach of young people to sex a healthy reaction against these old viewpoints?

It is clear that we shall not create change in our moral climate by an attempt to resuscitate the old authoritarian arguments. Neither the words of the Bible, nor the teachings of the Church, are likely to make much impact on young people, apart from the minority who accept unquestioningly the validity of religious teaching. Neither can we expect the moral dictates of the older generation to be accepted by boys and girls who have a growing suspicion that their elders do not always practise what they preach.

VALID TRUTHS AND TRADITIONS

This is not to say that the insights of the Bible and the Church are irrelevant. On the contrary, they contain great truths which will always be valid. Nor is the authority which comes from experience to be dismissed entirely, for parents and teachers are still frequently wiser than their offspring and pupils! All that is permanently valid in the moral traditions of the past must today be given to the younger generation in a manner which is non-authoritarian and in a language which is non-ecclesiastical.

How can this be done?

The point was made again and again in the Newsom Report that 'boys and girls need to arrive at some code of moral and social behaviour which is self-imposed', and it added in a useful chapter on 'Spiritual and Moral Development':

> Most boys and girls want to be what they call 'being good' and they want to know what this really implies in the personal situation which confronts them. They want also to know what kind of an animal man is, and whether ultimately each one of them matters and, if so, why and to whom. And they want to be told the truth.[1]

YOUTH ARTICULATE

Despite charges which are sometimes made to the contrary, many young people today face life with a sense of responsibility which was not always so obvious in previous generations. Even student protests that sometimes seem irresponsible in their extravagance are intended to be a serious response from the growingly articulate generation to the political and social problems of the world in which they are growing up. It is well known that social responsibility projects play an increasingly important part in schools and youth clubs. When the challenge to be responsible is effectively presented to them, many boys and girls are ready to make a valid response. Sexual ethics must therefore be presented to young people today in terms not of prohibition but of personal responsibility. And such responsibility has to be seen at different levels. On the level of the prevention of venereal disease, everything must be done to put the facts before boys and girls fairly and squarely. Once the facts are clearly seen, many will see the irresponsibility of risking the infection of oneself, or of passing it on either to the sexual partner or to the unborn child. Can schools and youth organizations claim that everything is now being done to disseminate

[1] *Half our Future.* A Report of the Central Advisory Council for Education (England), H.M.S.O., 1963, p. 52.

the necessary information, and so inculcate a sense of responsibility even at this level? And how much is this a matter of Christian concern?

Of course, the majority of young people are not concerned with casual promiscuity. They want to know the reasons why they should not go 'all the way' with the steady boy or girl friend. And rightly (or wrongly) V.D. does not seem to them to come into the picture. But the possibility of an unwanted pregnancy cannot be left out of the argument. Research shows that in a large number of pre-marital relationships contraceptives are not used. And when they are used, they may not prove reliable. These are facts which should also be bluntly stated. But, of course, young people have a right to reply, 'If the only reason you can give for chastity is the possibility that a baby may be conceived, why don't you provide us with reliable contraceptive information?' This is a valid point, and a reasonable case can be made for providing effective contraceptive advice to young men and women who by deliberate choice decide to have intercourse before marriage. For once a couple have come to this decision, they have a moral obligation to choose the best possible means to avoid conception. This is responsible moral advice which we should give to teenagers, even at the risk of being accused of leading the young astray. We must recognize that there are different levels of moral responsibility. There are morals within morals. The decision by the Family Planning Association to give contraceptive advice to unmarried young people who ask for it should therefore be welcomed by Christians whose concern for morality is matched by their fear of hypocrisy.

But, as every youth worker knows, many boys and girls want to press the point further. It is easy for them to recognize the dangers of disease and illegitimacy, if the facts are squarely presented. But once these fears are eliminated, what other reasons for chastity remain? This is the 64,000 dollar question which Fifth Formers and even Fourth Formers frequently raise. Discussions in recent years in conferences and organizations make it clear that there is little noticeable difference here between the attitude of young people who call themselves Christians and belong to the Church, and those who do not.

Here again the key word must be responsibility. Most (though not yet all) young people have a reasonable knowledge of the facts of sexual intercourse. Film strips and diagrams in the class-room have acquainted many of them with the physical nature of the act. But how much information are they given about the personal significance of sexual play and relationships? Are they helped to understand that when two people come together this is a relationship of whole persons and not just of certain bodily organs? It is here that so much sex education remains sadly defective. This is because warnings about the dangers of sex have played a far greater part in our instruction of the young than a positive approach to the understanding of the nature of sex. What is needed is not sex instruction, but education in the meaning of men and women in the relationship with one another. There is a fascinating section in the Newsom Report which deals with the teaching of science:

> The difference between knowing the facts and in some measure committing oneself to a personal attitude about their bearing on one's own actions stands out most clearly in that part of the science curriculum which deals with sexual reproduction ... whatever doubts and hesitations teachers in our schools may have about positive moral teaching, surely they will not doubt that one of the corner-stones of civilized existence is the principle that nobody, merely for his own ends, has rights in the life of another.[1]

TAKING SEX SERIOUSLY

One of the major obstacles to effective education is the

[1] *op. cit.*, p. 147.

contemporary trivialization of the sex relationship. This is evident in much popular writing, television and cinema. It is even more evident in the present convention in which young people, with little or no knowledge of one another as persons, indulge in heavy petting. This is a failure to take sex seriously. And a genuine sexual morality depends on taking sex seriously, precisely because it takes people seriously.

But here we have to be careful of the words we use. To say that we must take sex seriously is not an invitation to long-faced solemnity. Couples preparing for marriage need to be told that sex is fun, even though popular marriage manuals still tend to describe the sex relationship as if it were a rather pompous mixture of physiology and jujitsu! The writers of these books often lack that spontaneous sense of humour which is probably more essential to happy marriage than the technical information which they so solemnly impart.

Nevertheless, when a boy and girl indulge in sexual activities, whether or not they go 'all the way', they are doing something serious to one another as persons. This is something they must be helped to understand.

If they are using one another as partners in an experiment, or because 'everyone does it', or as a form of exploitation, this is to use sex in an irresponsible and even sub-human way. For this reason much pre-marital sex experience tends to be detrimental to marriage when it eventually comes. Not infrequently, married couples look back on their courtship days and regret they let their feelings run away with them. Yet we must be cautious about building up a morality too strongly on this kind of evidence. For while pre-marital experience undoubtedly frustrates some couples in their search for mutual fulfilment in marriage, there are others who will claim that sex experience before marriage helped rather than hindered their subsequent marital relationship.

GENUINE LOVE

But what we are bound to say to young people is that moral decision about sex behaviour must be made honestly and responsibly on the basis of taking both other people and ourselves with complete seriousness. This means that sex is debased when it is experienced outside the context of genuine love. Whether the real interests of love ever allow a full sexual relationship outside the total commitment of marriage is a matter on which opinions differ. It is difficult to be as dogmatic about this as Christians once thought it their duty to be. Certainly some sex relationships which take place outside marriage may be sacramental expressions of love and mutual commitment in a way which is lacking in other relationships within the bonds of marriage. The growing belief that moral questions such as this may be looked at situationally rather than prescriptively is not to throw morals overboard. It is to take morality with a deeper seriousness. As the *Sex and Morality* Report put it:

> We have not said that rules are valueless. We have tried to show that rules by themselves are an inadequate basis for morality. No rules can cover all the varied and complex situations in which men and women find themselves. Moreover an action which is in outward conformity with a rule may nevertheless be immoral because the motive and spirit behind it are wrong. Our reluctance to spell out the meaning of chastity in terms of basic rules is not due to any lack of conviction about the value of chastity, but rather to a desire to give adequate content to that word.[1]

It is certain that the approach to responsibility in human relations which has come to be known as the 'New Morality', far from being a twentieth century heresy, as some would have us believe, opens up the only way in which the morality of the New Testament will be understood in the future. It has been a great liberation from the

[1] *Sex and Morality*. A Report presented to the British Council of Churches, S.C.M. Press, 1966, p. 63.

very bondage of legalism and authoritarianism from which the New Testament itself proclaims release. Yet there is one aspect of this problem which has not yet received sufficient attention.

GUIDE LINES

What is the place of rules or guide lines in our presentation of morality today, and especially to the young? It is all very well (and right) to talk about situational ethics. But people sometimes need to be rescued from the worst side of their natures by simple guide lines. How do we present these without falling into the old ways which have so singularly failed to commend themselves? The *Sex and Morality* Report was 'reluctant to spell out the meaning of chastity in terms of basic rules', and many subsequent writers have shared that reluctance. Yet how certain can we be of our own maturity to do without rules? How much are we to be trusted? Even if we think we can dispense with schoolmasters, what about our responsibility to the younger generation?

The members of the Newsom Committee agreed that

> boys and girls should be offered firm guidance on sexual morality, based on chastity before marriage and fidelity within it.[1]

Many would agree with that. The question remains, How do you do it today? Does the Christian Gospel have anything to say apart from negative prohibitions and veiled warnings? It should at least be made clear to young people that the traditional Christian morality of chastity before marriage does not come from a fear of sex, or from a pious suspicion of anything which gives pleasure; but from a desire to take human love and its sexual expression with the seriousness it deserves. Despite our modern cynicism, it is the Christian and Jewish religion which has uniquely given a personal meaning to love.

[1] *Half our Future*, p. 55.

And it is precisely this deep inner personal meaning that the Church has been so successful in hiding!

When Dr. John Robinson (then Bishop of Woolwich) gave evidence at the Lady Chatterley trial (Regina versus Penguin Books Ltd.) he was widely reported and even more widely misunderstood. Yet what he had to say about the Christian understanding of sex was of great importance.[1] He quoted Archbishop William Temple who once said that Christians do not make jokes about sex for the same reason that they do not make jokes about Holy Communion, not because it is sordid, but because it is sacred, and he claimed that D. H. Lawrence was trying to portray this relation 'as in a very real sense something sacred, as in a real sense an act of Holy Communion'. If this profound Christian insight could be translated into the language which young people can understand, would not this help towards a new standard of morality in a way that commandments and exhortations can never do?

SEX IN MARRIAGE

In this respect, *Humanae Vitae* was a big step forward in the Roman Catholic Church. The view has been generally held (and not without reason) that Catholics were forbidden to think of the sex relationship other than as a means of procreation. That it also was an expression of love could not be denied, but it had to be seen as an additional bonus, and not as part of God's main purpose in the creation of sexuality. There have been times in Christian history when this viewpoint has been taken to absurd lengths. This is perhaps understandable when much of the traditional Christian theology of sex was laid down by celibate theologians, and the pastoral practice dictated in the confessional by unmarried priests. But even though *Humanae Vitae* continues (illogically, so it seems) the

[1] See *The Trial of Lady Chatterley*, ed. C. H. Rolph. Penguin Special, 1961.

traditional ban on artificial contraception, it attempts to give clear guidance on the meaning of sex as a personal relationship. It is a pity that so much attention has been paid to the prohibitive aspect of the Encyclical that its valuable positive teaching has been largely overlooked.

Conjugal love is described as fully human:

> that is to say, of the senses and of the spirit at the same time. It is not then a simple transport of instinct and sentiment but also, and principally, an act of free will, intended to endure and to grow by means of the joys and sorrows of daily life, in such a way that husband and wife become one only heart and one only soul, and together attain their human perfection.

> Then, this love is total, that is to say, it is a very special form of personal friendship, in which husband and wife generously share everything without undue reservations or selfish calculations. Whoever truly loves his marriage partner loves not only for what he receives, but for the partner's self, rejoicing that he can enrich his partner with the gift of himself.[1]

Despite the somewhat curious and stilted language, here is a high doctrine of the place of sex in marriage. And it is from this positive ideal that the value of chastity must be argued.

In a daring phrase, St. Paul likened the self-giving of a husband to his wife to the sacrifice of Christ for His Church: 'Husbands should love their wives just as Christ loved the Church and sacrificed himself for her to make her holy' (Eph. 5: 25).

But Christians have been slow to spell out the meaning of this for sexual relationship in the kind of language young people can really understand. The Church's warnings and prohibitions are clear enough. Its positive teaching has all too often been shrouded in the mystery of obscure or unintelligible language.

---

[1] 'On the Regulation of Birth.' Encyclical Letter of His Holiness Pope Paul VI, Catholic Truth Society, pp. 10–11.

For love means one-hundred per cent concern for the total well-being of the other person, whatever the cost to oneself. And it is with the word 'cost' that we come to the heart of the matter. Sacrifice lies at the root of all true relationship. And to place sexuality at the service of genuine love is to demand a self-control and an inner discipline which must not be weakened by half-baked ideas about repression drawn from popular psychology. Someone has said that it is not the Ten Commandments nor the Sermon on the Mount which is the basis of Christian morality. It is the Cross. And even those who cannot accept the Christian Creeds may not find it impossible to see love in terms of honest self-giving and the new life of freedom which comes out of discipline. It should be possibe for us to begin to work out an ethic along these lines in a language which communicates, and with an innate authority which commends itself.

A change of moral climate by a wistful attempt to resurrect the old authoritarianism or an appeal to fear can have no more than limited results. What is needed is an approach to education which presents sex fully and frankly in its relational context.

Here the meaning of responsibility to other people as persons needs to be fully worked out, and the whole range of responsible action to be honestly discussed. This must include a commendation of chastity as an expression of love and respect for the opposite sex and as a responsible preparation for marriage. It must also include a clear indication that the responsible use of contraceptives by those who (rightly or wrongly) decide to have intercourse before marriage is also a moral choice which must be made. There are responsible moral decisions to be made at every level of behaviour.

All this will not solve the problem completely. But is there any hope of changing the moral climate but by an approach to the education of boys and girls which is honest, open, non-authoritarian, non-pious, yet which

H

attempts to speak of the deepest Christian understanding of the gift of sex, and how it can and should be used with true responsibility?

II

In Britain, education was, by and large, pioneered by the Christian Church. The old grammar schools were generally associated with their local parish churches. Their aims were to promote godliness and sound learning. Their headmasters were almost invariably clergymen. Their annual Founders' Day Services are still a reminder – often the only reminder – of their pious beginnings. Popular education came much later, but again it was in the hands of the Church. In 1811 there was founded the National Society for the Education of the Poor in the Principles of the Established Church, fifty years before the first State Board Schools came into being. And with the establishment of schools, Christians began to see the necessity of having properly trained teachers. So the Church initiated teacher-training colleges. The first – the College of St. Mark and St. John – was opened as long ago as 1841. All this is a record of which the Church can be proud.

THE PRESENT SITUATION

But what of the present and the future? As a legacy of this early pioneering, the Church of England and the Roman Catholic Church today have a large network of schools as part of the national education system, and a not inconsiderable programme of church school building in many parts of the country. In the non-church schools, the religious origins of the education system are acknowledged by the provision of religious instruction according to an agreed syllabus, and by regular acts of worship at school assembly as laid down by the law of the land. Both churches still retain a good many colleges of education which, in common with the non-church ones, have been undergoing great changes in recent years both in size and in width of curriculum.

But is this a satisfactory pattern for the future? The British Humanist Association is fighting an increasingly intensive battle against the privilege which Christianity still enjoys, both in the time-table and in the management of our school system. But Humanists are not the only people to be worried about this. A growing number of Christians are beginning to ask whether the compulsory teaching of religious knowledge and the dual control of school management are really in the best interests of the Christian cause.

This is a subject on which it is hard to express an opinion without running the risk of engendering violently emotional reactions. Whenever the Church appears to be losing ground in the life of the community, Church people tend to cling to the visible props which still remain. They do not like letting go of their vested interests for fear that they will lose all points of evangelistic contact. So the religious programmes on radio and television are jealously guarded, as is the Church's stake in certain aspects of social work. But education, because the existing stake is so large and the bringing up of children is so important, is the vested interest where any suggestion of reform arouses the most suspicion. Do away with Church schools, abolish or broaden the religious education syllabus, and (so it is argued) we are throwing in the sponge and abandoning our country wholly to paganism. This is why (whatever may be their private views) very few of our Church leaders dare to voice critical opinions about this in public. It is best not to disturb sacred cows.

RELIGION IS LIFE

What are the problems? First, the syllabus of religious

instruction. There has been a welcome increase in the number of religious knowledge specialists in recent years, not least because women who read theology in the university are unlikely to find any other outlet for their skills in a male-dominated Church. But the fact remains that, by and large, religious knowledge, which is a highly specialized subject, is generally taught by non-specialists. Furthermore, religious knowledge is not just about the dates of the Kings of Israel or the itinerary of St. Paul's missionary journeys. It is a way of life. Even more than in the teaching of mathematics or history, the character and outlook of the teacher matter.

Precisely because it is a way of life, the wrong kind of religious knowledge teaching and experience in early days may do incalculable harm in a child's search for religious truth when in later life the quest becomes serious. To use the familiar image, incessantly repeated small doses of religion in childhood may successfully inoculate the child against catching the real thing later on. Modern educational research has made it clear how much damage can be done by religious teaching in early years. The pretty nativity plays which so delight the hearts of proud parents in infant and junior schools may actually make it more difficult for these same children to understand the stark and disturbing truth of the Incarnation of God in Christ when they come to teenage years. The Newsom Report *Half our Future* expressed sympathy with the bishop who told them in his evidence that he would scream if he ever saw any more camels on class-room walls.

It is essential to recognize that there are those who are seriously questioning what goes on under the name of religious education in infant and junior schools, and who are not doing so necessarily because they are either anti-religious or inconoclastic. They are doing it because they care desperately both for children and for the Christian cause.

ADOLESCENT RELIGION

When we consider the religious education of the adolescent there are other problems. It is clear that to omit religious instruction altogether during teenage would be to cut out a vital factor in the knowledge that any educated man should have. Whatever its truth or its falsity, the phenomenon of religion is one of the most persistent facts in the human situation. You cannot tell people about life, or equip them for it, without telling them about the questions men have always asked about ultimate meaning and purpose, and the various answers they have given throughout the centuries. And adolescents begin to ask the same basic questions that men have always asked, even though many of them find it hard to articulate them. Their growing concern with relationships in the spheres of sex, work, politics and social relationships, raises the great moral question which religion has always tried to answer. It may be doubted whether the kind of religious instruction which has one eye on the examination paper is likely to be of much help here. For the teenager, religious instruction must be closely geared into his own experience and his own questionings.

And surely the time has come when the answers which other religious systems have given should also be taught. It is not only unrealistic, but smacks of vested interest and privilege, if amongst all the answers people are giving today to life's problems, only the Christian one is officially acknowledged in school. Not only in our multi-racial society do we live alongside people who practise other religions, but there are also the humanist and the Marxist answers which need to be taken seriously if we are to take the world of today seriously. There is amongst many of the more intelligent young people a growing suspicion that the teaching of Christianity in schools has to be propped up by Act of Parliament for fear that it would not be able to stand on its own feet if left to fend for itself.

SCHOOL WORSHIP

The problem of school worship is also a difficult one. Its protagonists claim that compulsory attendance at Assembly gives to an increasing number of boys and girls their only experience of Christian worship. How can they make up their minds about a thing if they do not have a chance of experiencing it? If it were voluntary, the pressure of public opinion in a school would be to stay away from it, and the uncommitted would absent themselves (even if they felt like going) for fear of being branded as pious by the leaders of school opinion. This is an argument which cannot be lightly dismissed.

On the other hand, there is plenty of evidence to suggest that in far too many schools worship at Assembly does more harm than good. This is partly because it is often done without much imagination. There seems little reality in hymns and prayers which merely encourage the Establishment view of uplift, a view which is also dispensed by visiting speakers at the annual speech day. More seriously, the religious context of school Assembly is often that of established authority. School prayers are formal. The headmaster perhaps wears a gown here for the only time during the day. As soon as the prayers are over, various notices (some of an admonitory or disciplinary nature) are announced. Thus religion seems to be closely associated with the authoritarianism of the school set-up.

At an age when there is right and natural reaction to authority, religion is often discarded precisely because it seems to be there to uphold the prestige of the *status quo*. In a small way within the teenage outlook, the story of the Russian Revolution is being repeated. The Church is overthrown with the Tsars because it has got inextricably mixed up with them!

Here again there is no easy answer. Boarding-schools, where the problem is perhaps both more difficult and more easy, are beginning to experiment with voluntary in place of compulsory school chapel. At the moment the experiments are very tentative. Governors and old boys (many of whom probably do not go anywhere near church themselves today) dislike seeing the old pattern altered. In day-school, with varying success, heads are beginning to take their young people more and more into consultation about the content and leadership of school worship. Folk-songs are sometimes sung in the place of the familiar hymns. Guitars are sometimes heard instead of piano or organ. Readings from Shelter or Christian Aid literature may sometimes take the place of the Scriptures. All this is good, for certainly, if boys and girls continue to be made to worship during school hours, they must be presented with a Christianity which makes sense in terms of the world as they know it, and not just be involved in a curious and archaic exercise. The debate will continue.

Whatever decisions are reached, Christians must not cling to their vested interests simply because they are terrified of what might happen were they to leave go of them. There are many countries where the Church is much stonger than it is in England and where it would be completely impossible to have either religious instruction or Christian worship within the school time-table. If these things were lost entirely here, it might not be the unmitigated disaster that some people imagine.

THE DUAL SYSTEM

What about the dual system of school control? It is said that in a church school religious instruction does not have to be carried on in a vacuum. It can be closely associated with the life of a worshipping community. This is its strength, and it would be churlish to deny that there are parishes where the relationship between the school community and the local worshipping community is close and creative. Yet the awkward problems remain. If a really expert and long-term survey could be taken of children educated in church schools, and the influence of that education on them in later life, it is doubtful whether there would be very much evidence to suggest more positive influences at work than would be seen from their contemporaries educated in State schools. It is doubtful whether most local churches which have a school attached to them can show any great superiority in church membership or attendance, once the children have grown up. Putting it at its lowest, it has to be asked whether the vast sums which the Church of England spends on its church schools can really be shown to be giving value for money. It sometimes looks as though this money is paid out by Anglicans in order to keep up with the Roman Catholics. But some Roman Catholics are themselves beginning to doubt the value of their own church schools.

The more serious question is whether the dual system represents any longer the sort of way the Church ought to be involved in society. Is this the way the Church should carry on her mission in the world? Or is this really a form of ecclesiastical colonialism? We no longer feel that there ought to be church trade unions or church political parties. Is there really any justification for claiming a sector of the national education system for the Church? Are we not to be concerned with the whole of life? The whole of education? The whole political and social and industrial system in which we live? Can we really think that we make a greater contribution to education by opting out of the State system? And may we not, by doing so, be actually jeopardizing the mission of the Church in the whole community? For must it not be within the national education system that Christian teachers should be doing their work and making their witness? Anything that is keeping them locked up within the Church orbit is denying to society the things that such Christian teachers have it in them to bring. By the same token, it must be

seriously asked whether the Church is justified in retaining
its stake in the colleges of education.

What then of specific Christian instruction? This is
surely the business of the Church to do in its own way and
in its own time, and it is this which is being most inadequately done. It is because energies and resources are
being poured into church schools and education colleges
that in many Churches religious education in parish and
congregation is hopelessly equipped and badly done. In
the majority of Church of England parishes, religious
education stops at 13 with Confirmation. Occasionally
there is a Bible class, and a few young people are kept in
the Church for a few years longer by being made Sunday
School teachers, usually before they have many clues
about what Christianity means. Diocesan youth chaplains
try their best with inadequate staff and resources. Better
work still is done by the Christian Education Movement,
though this is crippled by lack of funds and staff.

And when we consider adult education, in spite of the
encouraging signs which come from such things as The
People Next Door Campaign and parish life conferences,
we have to admit that we are only scratching the surface.

END CHURCH SCHOOLS AND COLLEGES?

If there were more money and more plant, the Church
could really get down to the work of religious education in
this country. And where else can this money be found
except by relinquishing all claims on church schools and
education colleges? With these resources released, we
could provide the dioceses with larger and better trained
staffs of educational experts. Sunday Schools and Confirmation classes could be rescued from their present
amateur mediocrity into a highly professional educational
service geared into the real needs of today, and equipped
with the tools for the job. We could vastly increase the
resources of the Christian Education Movement, so that

its splendid work already being done in collaboration with State schools could be enlarged immeasurably. Recognizing the educational value of both residential work and travel in the religious education of teenagers, we could greatly increase the possibility of work camps, conferences, and inter-Church and international exchanges amongst young Christians. The experience of the German Evangelical Academies, and in this country of such places as William Temple College, the Iona Community, St. George's House, Windsor, and John Kennedy House in Coventry, proves the possibilities of a modern adult education programme. Such centres, in close collaboration with secular agencies, could be established in all key points in the country.

In fact, we need to be rescued from a narrow nineteenth century concept of religious education to one which is more in tune with the insights which have come to the Church afresh in our day. We have a Gospel of right relationships in a world at sixes and sevens with itself. We have the Gospel of Reconciliation in a divided world. We have a Gospel of Involvement in the rough and tumble of life. We should be less and less bothered whether the Church is seen to have a stake in the educational pattern or anywhere else. We should be more and more concerned that, by the very life of the Church in the world, we are enabling all men to live the more abundant life which is Christ's gift to us.

8

OUTLOOK ON WORSHIP

IN ENGLAND RECENTLY THE Roman Catholic Church
has translated the Mass into modern English with great
effect. The Church of England was less courageous. It
reformed the Liturgy, and it banished some of the more
obvious archaisms, but it retained a form of language
which, whilst reasonably dignified, remains old-fashioned
in flavour. Something can be said for retaining words and
sentences which link the present-day worshipper with the
Church of every age. Yet must historical perspective and
dignity necessitate a language of worship which suggests
that the God who is being approached is an archaism
rather than the Living Lord?

The casual visitor to the church must gain the impression that the business in hand has something to do with a
God who is alive. Much archaic language can be excused
neither on the grounds of history nor of dignity. It invades
our prayers, hymns, and even the rubrics which are
intended to be simple stage directions for the smooth
running of the drama of the liturgy. In a service for the
admission of Readers until very recently in use in Liverpool Diocese, the order began with this strange injunction:

> After Evensong, the sermon being ended, the Candidates
> duly habited and standing in their places shall be presented
> to the Bishop by the Warden with the words following
> (the congregation being seated).

A schoolboy who presented a Latin Prose translation
in that kind of stilted language would have his lesson
speedily returned! This kind of thing would be laughable
if it did not still happen in churches up and down the

land. Can anything be calculated so easily to confirm the visitor's suspicion that religion has nothing to do with real life? Nor can it be said that in those Free Churches which are not tied to archaic books of liturgy the situation is any better. You can still hear the collection announced as 'The stewards will now wait upon you for your alms'. Similarly the language of extempore prayer is often as stilted and antiquated as that of the set collects, and usually much more verbose. The best of the traditional prayers are often simple in language, and economical in construction, but too often they fail to create the visual image without which most people find it hard to make prayer a reality.

HYMN TYRANNY

Hymns are a special difficulty. Many of the best loved have a familiarity which disguises their unintelligibility. How many of the faithful have much of a clue what they mean when they sing:

> Thou spread'st a table in my sight;
> Thy unction grace bestoweth;
> And oh, what transport of delight
> From thy pure chalice floweth!

If that popular hymn has at least the merit of some relationship with the twenty-third psalm of which it is a paraphrase, others do not even have this to recommend them. You still hear congregations giving voice to:

> Bring your harps and bring your odours,
> Pour the strain and sweep the lay.

Nor is this made much more palatable by the substitution in some modern hymn-books of incense for odours!

BIBLE IN MODERN ENGLISH

There is a desperate shortage of good modern hymns, though not of other songs suitable for church use. But there is no shortage of modern versions of the Bible. The pioneer work of J. B. Phillips (who helped many people for the first time to see the New Testament as a living book) has been followed by the New English Bible, and more recently by the Jerusalem Bible with its magnificent translation of the Old Testament. It is curious that with these aids to making the Bible intelligible probably more churches continue to read the Scriptures aloud during service in the Authorized Version than from a modern translation.

Some time ago the House of Clergy of the Convocation of York discussed for an hour whether or not the Jerusalem Bible should be permitted in public worship in the Anglican Churches of the Province. After a somewhat fruitless discussion someone had resort to the time-honoured ecclesiastical device of moving that 'The question be not put'. This was thankfully accepted and the leaders of the Church moved to an equally thrilling discussion about the publication of Banns of Marriage! It seems crazily perverse for a Church which has been entrusted with the proclamation of the Gospel to refuse to read the Bible in the language most likely to help the congregation to get some idea of what the original author was trying to say. (See page 144.)

RELEVANCE

But it is not only a question of language. What lies behind the words? The Christian Faith is about relationships: Man's relationship with his God, and with his neighbour. This double relationship is articulated in public worship. Christians meet together to express what it means to belong to God, to one another, and to the world. How much of this concern is apparent in our acts of worship? Although we come to offer our prayers and praises to the God who revealed Himself 'once upon a time' in Jesus Christ, we must plant our worship firmly in the here and now. When the section of Uppsala said that 'Bible texts should be chosen that people are helped to worship with understanding',[1] it meant that they should not only know what the passage meant, but how it fitted into the general theme of the worship for the day. The Bible is not a magic charm dispensing automatic blessings so long as a prescribed number of verses are read aloud each week. The prayers should help the congregation to link together their picture of God with the reality of the world as it appears to them in the newspaper headlines and the television news each day. Even now it is possible to attend a service and get no clue in what century, let alone in what year or day, the worship is taking place! This is not to experience timelessness: it is sheer obscurantism. Intercession and petition are not escapes into some strange world of vague ideals. They are the way in which we focus the attention upon the political, social and personal facts of life within the context of God's mercy and judgment. Books like Michel Quoist's *Prayers of Life*[2] and Malcolm Boyd's *Are you running with me, Jesus?*[3] though not to be slavishly copied, indicate the kind of way corporate prayer can be led today.

Hymns provide an even more difficult problem of relevance, and it is hard not to conclude that the great popularity of hymn singing programmes on television and radio lies in the fact that people like to use their religion as a means of escape. Further, it is almost impossible to find hymns which can be used to express the Christian concern before God for the real problems of the world. Too many of those still to be found in the hymn-books are pleas for personal salvation ('Let me to thy bosom fly') rather than the songs of those who have been entrusted by their Lord with the ministry of reconciliation. Perhaps the best modern hymns are those sung by folk-singers. They have come out of a genuine anguish about

---

[1] *The Uppsala 68 Report*, S.C.M. Press, 1968, p. 81.
[2] Gill, Dublin.
[3] S.C.M. Press.

the nuclear threat, world hunger and poverty, and colour
discrimination. Those who saw on television the funeral
of Dr. Martin Luther King will never forget the continuous
sound of 'We shall overcome' as the procession wound its
way along the streets. This song of the freedom marchers
has the genuine quality possesed by the greatest of the
Psalms: a quality lacking from all but a very few of the
hymns we sing today.

Sydney Carter has done much to provide what the
traditional hymnody lacks. His words are usually very
simple. They are deeply informed by the Bible, but they
speak of today. A good example is his song, *Standing in
the Rain*, which relates the 'no room at the inn' theme
with our modern prejudices and weaknesses:

> No use knocking on the window,
> There is nothing we can do, Sir,
> All the beds are booked already –
> There is nothing left for you, Sir.
>
> No use knocking at the window,
> Some are lucky, some are not, Sir,
> We are Christian men and women,
> But we're keeping what we've got, Sir.
>
> No, we haven't got a manger,
> No, we haven't got a stable,
> We are Christian men and women
> Always willing, never able.
>
> Jesus Christ has gone to heaven;
> One day he'll be coming back, Sir.
> In this house He will be welcome,
> But we hope He won't be black, Sir.

Fred Kaan has done a modern paraphrase of the
Magnificat. It lacks the poetry of the familiar words, but
the essentially revolutionary character of Mary's words
(generally hidden when sung in the context of Choral

Evensong or a Mothers' Union Festival) comes out splendidly in the first and last verses:

> Sing we a song of high revolt
> Make great the Lord, His name exalt.
> Sing we the song that Mary sang
> Of God at war with human wrong.
>
> *   *   *   *
>
> He calls us to revolt and fight
> With him for what is just and right,
> To sing and live Magnificat
> In crowded street and council flat.

These are two examples out of many: and they are encouraging. For some time bodies like the Twentieth Century Church Light Music Group have been experimenting with new tunes, some of which have been successful, and others have been distressingly like a decadent mixture of Moody, Sankey and Ivor Novello! But more urgent than twentieth-century tunes is the need for twentieth-century words, and the Folk Song movement has opened our eyes to the possibility of a modern hymnody.

They asked at Uppsala whether fresh categories of people should not find a place in the Church's prayers? As instances, they mentioned industrial workers, students and scientists. But the Church must not only pray *for* these and other categories of people; it must also pray *with* them.

INVOLVEMENT

When doctors, students, or members of a social service organization or Insurance Institute come to church for worship, they should not get the impression that they are privileged to share in what somebody else is doing for them. They must themselves feel involved. They must sense that the hymns, readings and prayers bring the Word of God to them in their own situation. Otherwise they will be conscious only of having taken part in an irrelevant ceremony, adding little significance to their work and interests other than a touch of respectability.

When the Church tries seriously to involve different sections of the community in its worship, it discovers one of the most effective means of fulfilling its mission today. For worship which has been carefully prepared to meet a particular situation not only helps to make the Word incarnate in the life of the community, it also demonstrates that the Church cares more for the world than for itself.

This is why liturgical rigidity can be so damaging. If a Church insists on having Choral Eucharist when the Mayor and Corporation come, because it happens to be the third Sunday of the month, it displays a rigid legalism and concern for its own correctness which has little to do with the Gospel of love. Many thousands of young people must have been put off public worship for good and all as a result of having to endure a church parade where sung Evensong (with set lessons, psalms and the lot) suggested to them that the church authorities had hardly noticed that they were in the congregation. Flexibility and adaptability in worship must be part of our understanding of mission. Those who insist on keeping all the rules in the book, whoever may be in the congregation, are showing that they believe that the world exists for the Church, and not the reverse.

But if there is to be real communication in worship, those who are responsible for the conduct of worship must take the views and concerns of the worshippers seriously. If the City Council or a youth organization is due to attend church for a special service, the clergy should recognize that careful consultation with the representatives of these bodies is as much part of preparation for worship as the composing of the sermon or the rehearsing of the anthem. What are the things which the organization particularly wants to give thanks to God for? Where are the failures and shortcomings for which

I

penitence should be encouraged? What are the hopes and fears upon which intercessions can be built? And to what passages of Scripture should we turn for the particular inspiration and guidance which this organization needs at this moment in its history? Laity are often surprised, and sometimes even slightly embarrassed, at being consulted about worship by the clergy; but it is the only way to turn formal religious ceremony into active mission.

APPROACH TO CHILDREN

For a long time 'mission services' have played a large part in the difficult work of children's evangelism, but they have often presented the faith in a picture language which makes little sense to boys and girls growing up in an industrial society. However dear such hymns are to the hearts of Sunday School teachers, the picture language of 'Loving Shepherd of thy sheep' seems weak and sentimental to the modern city child. It has little to do with the exciting world of 'The Avengers', 'The Man from Uncle', or top league football on their television programmes. So we in Liverpool tried to present in both Biblical and contemporary terms the modern mission of the Church in an act of worship at which three thousand boys and girls were present.

The focal point of the service was to be the handing in of gifts for the work of a hospital in Lagos. The theme was to be the Christian mission in the world of today, pictured as the fight against evil. To many boys and girls today, the scene conjured up by the word 'fight' is that of a boxing or wrestling match, such as they see on television. This links with St. Paul's picture of the Christian athlete: 'I am like a boxer who does not beat the air.' It was decided to build the act of worship around a visual presentation of the Christian fight in the world. In the centre of the cathedral was a boxing ring. After a preliminary hymn and a Bible reading, the children were told to sit down for the sermon. But they were told that, instead of this being preached from the pulpit, the sermon was going to be acted in the boxing ring.

Then followed a four-round contest in which Johnny Christian fought in turn with Billy Ignorance, Harry Hunger, Davey Disease and Cassius Comfort. A running commentary linked the language of the boxing ring with the task of the Church in the world. It included a surprising amount of information about poverty, disease, illiteracy, superstition, and the unequal distribution of the world's resources. It showed how the Christian mission is deeply involved in a solution of these problems. Johnny Christian did not have it all his own way. From time to time he was nearly knocked out. At the end of the contest there was no clear decision; only the resolution to go on fighting. This was a far cry from the old success stories by which missionary societies used to solicit for donations.

Of course, the children participated vigorously in the proceedings. They were on the edge of their chairs with excitement. When there was a near knock-out, they joined loudly with the referee in the count. And the final round involved the children themselves. They brought their gifts for medical missions to Johnny Christian in the ring. They were sharing with him in the fight. Near the end of the service there was a period of intercession. Carefully the various aspects of the Christian mission, which had been dramatized in the fight, were turned into simple and direct prayer. The great congregation of children, who had been shouting and cheering during the boxing match were far more silent and concentrated in their attention than the average adult congregation at prayer time. This was because the 'acted sermon' had helped them to visualize vividly the ideas which were now being presented in prayer. Although some people were shocked, this was no gimmick. It was a legitimate use of drama within worship, and the positive response of the children was clear evidence that it had succeeded.

The Uppsala section on worship describes how the Church:

> as it moved into different cultures and ages, has incorporated elements from other sources. Art, drama and bodily postures have all been employed. The aim has been to reach men in the depth of their being, and to bring them to know the God and Father of Jesus Christ.[1]

NEW SYMBOLISM

We need to find new symbolism in worship, not least that which can be drawn from popular entertainment; but such symbolism must be used with intelligence, imagination and integrity. Part of the impact of the 'boxing match' service was that the children felt themselves to be caught up in the drama. They were actively participating. For too long public worship has been something which a handful of professionals at one end of the Church have done for the majority sitting at the other end. Yet often people have little vision of worship as a response to the relationship between God and man, and man and his neighbour, until they are involved in the creation of liturgy. To some extent the priest pontificating all alone, on behalf of those who are not allowed to do what he does, is a relic of the time when our concept of leadership was much less democratic than it is today. More and more, the priesthood of all believers needs to be expressed in terms of a worship in which all have a share.

Some time ago the Principal of a well-known college of physical education asked if there could be a carol service in Liverpool Cathedral for the staff, students and their friends. The suggestion was that it should be along the lines of the traditional Nine Lessons and Carols. But further discussion suggested that a college which specializes

[1] *op. cit.*, p. 80.

in dance, mime and physical activities should use its own specialities as the main ingredient in its Christmas worship.

After much discussion, involving both staff and students, three ten-minute dances were evolved. The first presented, in abstract form, the work of the prophets of the Old Testament: the story of courage in the face of opposition and rejection. The second took the main elements in the Christmas story, the Holy Family, the shepherds, the kings and the angels, and wove them into a glorious pattern of dance. The third was a dance symbolizing the fruits of the Spirit, signifying the difference which the coming of Christ into the world should make to human relationships. The three dances were set into a liturgical framework, including hymns and prayer. This was an act in which speech, dance, music and colour all combined to present the Bible story of God's purpose for mankind. It was deeply moving, but even more important was the impact it made on some of the students who took part.

In the process by which they had to think out the basic theological truths of the Christmas story, and then translate them into the language of choreography, they began to discover the deeper meaning of a faith which until now had never made any claim upon them. Some of them were prepared to say that this participation in the creation of worship was a conversion experience.

Perhaps every Church should become a workshop where groups of people are given free rein to hammer out the meaning of worship in the context of life as they know it. For there is little that liturgical committees can do as they discuss these things in a vacuum unless there is plenty of experiment of rich variety, taking place all over the country. Worship which arises out of corporate study and commitment, with the sharing of experience and talents, can become a powerful instrument of mission.

'Disgusted, disgusted, disgusted with the programme you

had on TV on Christmas Eve. To think of a most
beautiful cathedral brought down to these depths, a
programme suitable only for the Cavern', wrote a dis-
gruntled correspondent to a local paper. The object of
this fury was a fifty-minute presentation on television one
Christmas Eve. It was the alternative offering to the
traditional Carol Service from King's College, Cam-
bridge. 'It must have infuriated the Nine Lessons and
Carols traditionalists', wrote the *British Weekly* critic.
And he was right.

Anyone who has the responsibility for ordering public
worship knows the problem. On the one side is the
liturgical rut into which so many of us get stuck. On the
other side is the enticement of the latest gimmick. The
first of these is unsatisfactory to all except those whom
long years of churchgoing have lulled into insensitivity.
The second calls forth immediate howls of protest from
the large number of pew-sitters and television watchers
who, in matters of liturgical experiment, are on principle
against anything that is new. Gimmickry is dangerous.
But there must be experiments, and experiments far
more radical than those likely to be thought up by liturgical committees. What places are more suitable for such
experiments than cathedrals and the great central churches
with their resources of space, staffing, and flexibility?
What better medium than television with its production
teams expert in the craft of communication, and its
contract departments ready to hire worth-while artists on
a professional basis?

For a number of years there have been 'Pop' Christmas
Services for young people in Liverpool cathedral. They
have combined professional groups with local talent.
On each occasion nearly 3,000 boys and girls have come
to the cathedral. Nor was it difficult to give these services

a real theological dimension. Traditional carols and new compositions to lively 'beat' rhythms speak easily of the joy and exhilaration of the Christmas story. Many modern folk and protest songs tell more eloquently of our response to the 'Man for others' than most of the material to be found in the traditional hymn-books. Without claiming too much, it is certainly easier to get to the heart of the Incarnation message by using modern pop and folk music than it is by those medieval lullabies and cradle songs which are features of so many Christmas carol services both in schools and churches.

But the television production 'How on Earth?' attempted to break new ground. In the first place, it was a presentation designed especially for television, using the vast cathedral as a studio, and 2,500 young people as a studio audience. Further, it tried to tell the Christmas story by using a wide variety of media: pop and folk music, straight choral singing, drama, dance and audience participation and the spoken word, including the use of the local Liverpool dialect. It aimed at a mass audience at a peak viewing time, and hoped to get something of the Christmas Gospel across to those who would not be held by more traditional religious broadcasts. The synopsis of the programme was simple. A linking commentary, with a minimum of words, tried to indicate the significance of the sequence of events.

The programme began (as the Bible begins) with the World. The well-known Group, the Bee Gees, sang their latest number from the Top Twenty charts.

The commentary then intervened. Why pop music and dancing in a cathedral? Because long before Christians celebrated the birth of Christ, people kept the mid-winter festival. The Birth of Christ did not put an end to the dancing and singing. It gave it a new dimension.

Then followed the Gospel story of the birth of Christ read in local dialect by a Liverpool-born disc jockey. In response to this reading, the Settlers, an excellent Folk

Group, gave a lively account of 'The Virgin Mary had a baby boy'. During this, many of the young people in the cathedral started clapping and dancing. This was one of the most impressive parts of the broadcast. Dancing has always been associated with worship, and here it took its place quite unselfconsciously.

Next followed the sheep stealing scene from the Wakefield Christmas Mystery Plays. As the commentary pointed out, this was unashamed fifteenth-century pantomime (the shepherd's wife was played by a man) and showed how naturally Christians came to see the secular and the sacred as all of a piece.

The next item was intended to illustrate the same point. Following a reading of the Annunciation from the New English Bible, the cathedral choir sang a modern setting of the Magnificat into which the composer had woven South American rhythms. The New English Bible is normally read in the cathedral, and Brian Kelly's setting of the Magnificat is frequently sung by the cathedral choir. Two elements from normal cathedral worship were deliberately introduced here to show that experiments in Christian communication need not be entirely divorced from the regular pattern of Christian worship. Nor are they confined to the world of pop music.

At this point, a young Liverpool folk-singer shouted 'Stop' and against a filmed background depicting war, famine, homelessness and racial intolerance, sang:

> Since He came the world seems the same.
> Why on earth did He come?
> What on earth was the Saviour's game?
> Why on earth did He come?

And the commentary elaborated on this dark side of Christmas. Like millions of others, God's Son was born in a shack and became a refugee. Like millions of others, He was the victim of cruelty and injustice.

The broadcast finished on a note of dedication and

prayer. First the whole assembly swinging to 'If I had a Hammer', leading on to the quiet ending, with a young man standing alone on the nave bridge speaking the St. Francis prayer:

> Lord, make us instruments of your peace;
> Where there is hatred, let us sow love . . .

The programme was, on the whole, well received. The greatest appreciation came from those who had some knowledge of the younger generation and the concern to make the Gospel real for them. Letters of appreciation outnumbered letters of criticism. This is unusual, since protesters normally put pen to paper more quickly than appreciators. Yet there was some violent criticism, and it is clear that some people were genuinely shocked. A careful examination of the protests suggested that, by and large, these were based on *cultural* rather than theological grounds.

Typical was a letter from a well-meaning Liverpudlian in the local paper.

> The beauty and dignity, even the popularity of Liverpool cathedral are not enhanced by beat music rendered by youths badly in need of a hair cut. The sonorous tones of the great organ, playing music by Brahms, Schubert and Mendelssohn are what people of good taste and Christian sentiment want and expect.

Almost all the other critical letters received or published in the local Press took up the same theme. We were not making 'churchy' or 'cathedral' sounds. Therefore we were wrong. Truly our worship has become imprisoned in a middle-class culture, unable to communicate to the vast mass of people today.

If the Church is to be catholic in its attempt to proclaim the Christian message, it must not be tied to one single cultural pattern. The same principle is true for those who are concerned with the presentation of religious truth through the medium of television. That is why this kind of programme must be seen in the context of the total schedules both of the Church and television broadcasting at Christmas time. There is no lack of traditional carol services, recitals, nativity plays and acts of worship in our churches and schools. But without radical experiments in the more popular media, we ignore a large section of the community in our presentation of worship.

The theme throughout this book has been that the Christian Gospel brings good news of relationships. God's relationship with man, and man's relationship with his neighbour, are inextricably linked. This two-fold relationship is dramatized as nowhere else in the Holy Communion.

It is an act of communion with God and an act of communion with our neighbour. Neither communion makes sense without the other.

THE DOUBLE ASPECT OF COMMUNION

One of the most heartening facts of the modern ecumenical scene is that Churches of many traditions are making simultaneous and similar discoveries about the meaning of the Eucharist as they move forward in liturgical reform. Not long ago, Roman Catholics and Protestants would have found the experience of attending the Sacrament in one another's churches bewildering and largely meaningless. Now we are all beginning to speak with much the same language, and to feel at home in each other's churches. And in every Church, Eucharistic renewal has been primarily directed towards making the double aspect of communion more real – the Godward and the manward.

The two new cathedrals in Liverpool illustrate this point. In the Anglican cathedral, the high altar with its accompanying reredos is of great beauty and magnificence. It is against the east wall of the building, and the focal point of an immense chancel. Above it is a vast window illustrating the Te Deum. It is far away, breathtaking and unusable. A movable nave altar, capable of being placed anywhere in the cathedral, is used for the celebration of the Sacrament. Nevertheless the high altar is more than a focal point in the architecture. It speaks of the transcendence of God: His 'otherness'. It invokes that sense of reverence and awe which is an essential part of worship. But for the celebration of Holy Communion it is impracticable.

In contrast, the high altar in Gibbard's splendid Roman Catholic metropolitan cathedral is in the centre of the circular building. The seats are all around, and the table is in the centre of a circular sanctuary, not unlike a circus ring. Although, as at Coventry and other cathedrals, it is not always possible for the congregation to see what is happening at the altar, yet when a great congregation is assembled for Mass there is a feeling of 'togetherness around the table' which the Nonconformist architect clearly intended. Whilst the architecture in the Anglican cathedral speaks of the transcendence of God, that of the Roman Catholic cathedral testifies to His immanence.

Neither building provides a complete answer to the liturgical problem, and in each the clergy have to use their ingenuity to overcome some of the limitations which the architecture imposes. It would seem that to do justice, not only to the many-sidedness of the Eucharist, but also to the changing liturgical emphasis from one generation to another, architects must provide buildings of the maximum flexibility. Certainly, the present stress on 'the God in the midst' may be counterbalanced in due course by a desire to emphasize again the otherness of God. Both elements are essential in our understanding of worship, and particularly in the celebration of the Eucharist.

Uppsala, in drawing attention to the early Christian tradition of celebrating the Eucharist every Sunday, urged a return to what many Christians always considered the norm.[1] This is the typical act of Christian worship. This is what Christians are expected to do when they come together on the Lord's Day. Yet attention might also have been drawn to the dangers of over-frequent communion, and particularly of those week-day celebrations which are only attended by the priests (who, in a sense, are paid to do this kind of thing), and the very devout laity. The danger of this practice is that it tends to turn the Eucharist into a kind of snack bar for the pious minority. The Supper Table is supposed to be spread for the whole Christian community as it comes to meet its Lord in the breaking of bread. In the Church of England people can still be heard talking about 'making my communion', which is a contradiction in terms. The small number who went to 'early service', or who 'stayed behind' after Matins spread themselves at a safe distance from one another all over the church.

But the Eucharist is not primarily a place where the individual can meditate on the meaning of the passion. It is the place where the Church learns to be the Church in the world. It is for this reason that Churches which have put less than due emphasis on Communion within their scheme of worship are beginning to give it greater place. And Churches where frequent non-communicating attendance has been the practice are now beginning to move towards the Uppsala recommendation that 'all Christians present at the Eucharistic Service should normally take part in Holy Communion'. For when people communicate together they are saying as much about their relationship with one another as they are about their relationship with God. Certainly, in the Anglican tradition, the

[1] *op. cit.*, p. 82.

individualistic view of Holy Communion has been so
stressed that it was considered almost irreverent to take
too much notice of your neighbour in church, and especially at the Holy Communion. Little booklets given to the
newly confirmed would preface the act of consecration
with the words 'now we come to the most sacred part
of the service, do not look about you'. So most of us
grew up learning to peep through our fingers with a
slight sense of guilt at 'the most sacred moment of the
service'.

If our worship is to be true to the basic insights of the
Bible, we should be aware of our communion with God
and our communion with our fellow-men at one and the
same time. To separate them is to break the essential link
between them on which the Bible insists throughout.

INVOLVEMENT OF THE LAITY

The corporate nature of the Eucharist has been stressed
in recent years by the greater involvement of the laity,
particularly in the Churches which have been traditionally priest-centred. For instance, at the Mass of Consecration of the metropolitan cathedral in Liverpool, a
layman not only read the epistle but also led the intercessions. In the Church of England, laymen are beginning
to take a greater share in the service, including preaching
and the distribution of the elements. There remains an
absurd regulation which prohibits women preaching at
Holy Communion, but it will slowly and inevitably come
to be that both the Ministry of the Word and of the Sacrament are seen as the joint responsibility of priest and
laity together.

It is, perhaps, in the leadership of intercession within
the Eucharist that the layman has his most distinctive
part to play. For this double act of communion with God
and with men has within it a third element: a deep concern for the world. As the layman can represent in his own

person, as well as by his words, the weekday involvement of the congregation in the life of the community around. For it must be the real concern of the workaday world which Christians have in their hearts and consciences as they seek to understand the meaning of communion with God and with each other. Otherwise, the Eucharist itself becomes an escape from the world, rather than a demonstration to the world how, in obedience to God, the divisions which disintegrate the human situation can be healed. What is demonstrated, as Christians kneel together to receive the common things of life charged with new power and meaning by the grace of God, must be taken out of the sanctuary and translated into the language of politics, economics and society.

THE SCANDAL OF DIVISION

And it is just here that the divisions of the Church, even at the Lord's Table, become the great scandal. How can we dare tell the world that we have been entrusted with the message of reconciliation when we continue to demand passports with appropriate visas before admitting others to or being received ourselves at one another's communion tables. Arguments about apostolic succession and valid ministries seem to the world to be irrelevant and unconvincing. They look like the demarcation disputes which create inter-union rivalry and make a mockery of the brotherhood of workers. And what is bad or disruptive in industry becomes blasphemous in the Church. We are like marriage guidance counsellors who are themselves guilty partners in a divorce case. We speak about unity with our lips, and deny it with our lives. And worse still, we deny it at the very place we dare to call the Holy Communion. Even today, when great ecumenical gatherings are held in a spirit of splendid brotherhood, the various denominations tend to arrange separated communion services to which their own members can hive off.

The facts of the situation either demand full inter-communion without further ado, or a Eucharistic Fast in which all share as a sign of their unworthiness to share in any activity which dares to call itself Communion. Jesus said to his disciples, 'If you are bringing your offering to the altar, and there remember that your brother has something against you, leave your offering there before the altar, go and be reconciled with your brother first, and then come back and present your offering' (Matt. 5: 23, 24).

Does this mean that we should either give up the pretence of Holy Communion until all those who follow Christ can come to it freely together, or that we should take immediate steps to break down the barriers at the ecclesiastical frontiers? If we are called to be ministers of reconciliation in this divided world, is not the full expression of Christian communion at the Lord's Supper an absolute first priority? Are there really any principles important enough to keep us in separation when the overriding principle of love compels us to come together?

It may be that Churches remain in separation because they are at heart more interested in themselves than they are in either Christ or in the world. And if this is so, the outlook remains unsettled. Are we not being called in the Churches to take both Christ and the world with a new seriousness? Ineffectiveness lies in the middle path which steers clear of total commitment to Christ and total involvement in the world. The mission of the Church in our day, as in every generation, is so to discover what it means to care for the world that we are compelled to take Jesus at His word; and so prepared to take Jesus at His word that we are driven back into the world to work out in practical terms what it means to be entrusted with the good news of right relationships.

Note to section on

BIBLE IN MODERN ENGLISH

In October 1969 (as this book was going to press) the Convocations of Canterbury and York approved a motion authorizing the reading of the Jerusalem Bible in the Church of England.